AKASHVANI

Advance Praise for *Akashvani*

'All India Radio has played a stellar role in preserving and nurturing classical music since Independence. Most classical musicians of the day owe AIR a huge debt of gratitude for support during their days of struggle. Neelesh Kulkarni and Vikrant Pande have written an immensely readable tribute to this venerable institution.'

—Padma Bhushan Vishwa Mohan Bhatt, musician, inventor and an acclaimed player of the Mohan Veena

'In this age of social media, the internet and television, if Neelesh Kulkarni and Vikrant Pande have penned a book on the influence and contribution of radio, I would rate it a brave effort. Somebody had to do it—and Neelesh and Vikrant have done it with rare authenticity. Written in their well-known catchy style, this book will attract experts as well as commoners. Congratulations!'

—Padma Shri Sushil Doshi, journalist, author and sports commentator

'"*Sakhee sahelii ...*" The cheerful promo voice chirps to ring in the hour-long programme dedicated to the women of India. *Sangeet Sarita* is a comforting flow via megahertz into millions of homes that may not have ever learnt sangeet. Akashvani and its iconic programmes are celebrities in their own right, which have earned loyalty in the age of fickle audience attention. This is an important book and a fascinating read. Kudos to Vikrant Pande and Neelesh Kulkarni for factually and meticulously chronicling the story of India's most-loved radio service—from the Mahatma speaking into the microphone to an AIR app today for the young. All the best to the authors—though I am jealous that they wrote a book on what I could have as a broadcaster myself!'

—Vasanthi Hariprakash, award-winning radio show host, journalist and entrepreneur

'Akashvani is a living memory of modern democratic India marching on its developmental journey. From PM Modi's *Mann ki Baat* to Vividh Bharati's *Jaimala*, its programmes and stories echo through its airwaves, blending the ancient and the modern, seeking relevance in the age of the internet, smartphone and artificial intelligence. Neelesh Kulkarni and Vikrant Pande have written an immensely readable account of this journey. I recommend it to all.'

—Shashi Shekhar Vempati, former CEO of Prasar Bharati, technocrat and media professional

AKASHVANI
A Century of Stories from
ALL INDIA RADIO

Vikrant Pande and
Neelesh Kulkarni

HarperCollins *Publishers* India

First published in India by HarperCollins *Publishers* 2025
4th Floor, Tower A, Building No. 10, DLF Cyber City,
DLF Phase II, Gurugram, Haryana – 122002
www.harpercollins.co.in

2 4 6 8 10 9 7 5 3 1

Copyright © Vikrant Pande and Neelesh Kulkarni 2025

P-ISBN: 978-93-6569-973-9
E-ISBN: 978-93-6569-891-6

The views and opinions expressed in this book are the authors' own
and the facts are as reported by them, and the publishers
are not in any way liable for the same.

Vikrant Pande and Neelesh Kulkarni assert the moral right
to be identified as the authors of this work.

All rights reserved. No part of this publication may be reproduced,
stored in a retrieval system, or transmitted, in any form or by any means,
electronic, mechanical, photocopying, recording or otherwise,
without the prior permission of the publishers.

Typeset in 11.5/15 Bembo Std at
HarperCollins *Publishers* India

Printed and bound at
Thomson Press (India) Ltd

MIX
Paper | Supporting
responsible forestry
FSC® C010615

This book is produced from independently certified FSC® paper
to ensure responsible forest management.

To
Shri Datta Kulkarni, the voice of Marathi news for forty years

CONTENTS

Authors' Note	*ix*
1. The Beginning	1
2. The Spoken Word: The News	17
3. The Spoken Word: Sports Commentary	44
4. The Spoken Word: Plays, Poetry and Stories	64
5. The Spoken Word and the Mixed Format	81
6. The Mixed Format: Ads and Jingles	92
7. Music: Indian Classical	108
8. Music: Vividh Bharati	130
9. Music: Western	155
10. The Future	166
Author's Musings: Vikrant Pande	*199*
Author's Musings: Neelesh Kulkarni	*201*

Authors' Note

WHEN WE BEGAN RESEARCHING ALL INDIA RADIO (AIR), IT was clear that its omnipresence was unquestioned. Our quest, however, was to explore the depth and width to which AIR existed, not just in people's subconsciousness but also in today's reality. Was it as popular as we imagined or dying as many confidently claimed? The only way to find out was to dive deep into it.

Was AIR a habit people merely tolerated or was it something they actively tuned in to? We wanted to know the answers to these so badly that we began this journey. What started as a curiosity soon turned into a passion. We met people from walks of life we had never imagined or expected to meet. They included advertising professionals, ghazal singers, classical musicians, radio jockeys, commentators, chai wallahs, dhaba owners, lawyers and CEOs. It was a journey that took us to many parts of India, in which one question led to another and each answer stoked our curiosity further.

Researching AIR's history took us to meet people who had previously worked with the medium, those who shape its destiny today and those who have been observing it for years. They gave us unknown insights and enriched this book with their anecdotes.

Each meeting left us thirsty to explore more. So many people contributed their knowledge, information and experiences to this book that just thanking them with a sentence each would mean adding an entire chapter to this book.

When we met these diverse listeners from different walks of life, we realized AIR's Vividh Bharati was not the only offering from the public broadcaster attracting mass adulation. There were die-hard news listeners as loyal as those glued to the sports commentary on AIR while watching the very same match on TV! Some people would not miss the classical music programmes for anything, while others enjoyed the whole world of jingles and hummed them while driving or cooking. That Vividh Bharati and its programmes have legendary fan clubs is well known. We also discovered that its decades-old yet evergreen programmes like *Sangeet Sarita*, *Sakhi Saheli*, *Jaimala* and *Bhule Bisre Geet*, to mention a few, continue to draw millions of listeners.

Surprisingly, AIR fans are not just from the tier-two and tier-three towns of Jhumri Telaiya or Bhatapara, but its fan base cuts across gender, income and age groups. The reach of AIR is an advertiser's delight and its diversity is a corresponding nightmare!

We discovered that *Sakhi Saheli*, a programme targeted at women, has a huge male fan following while lakhs of people who have no desire to learn classical music listen to *Sangeet Sarita*. We realized that the sheer magic of the presenters and the rich content of these programmes drive millions to it. The innate simplicity of the presentation, the modesty of the RJs who otherwise have cult status and the sheer familiarity that the listener feels with AIR drive the connection that listeners have with it. Presenters told us hundreds of stories of how listeners calling from all parts of India express this.

However, the fascinating forays emerged when we dove deep into the modernization process. We discovered that five million people listen to radio on their mobile phones through the News On Air app, twenty million subscribe to the YouTube channels and countless others connect on the websites, Twitter handles and Facebook pages. We learned about the forays into the digital world and how they were poised to revolutionize news and create and store varied content. With the technical innovations backing up a humongous amount of talent, we realized as we progressed on the book's journey that the future was rosy.

We began with nostalgia in mind, were enthralled with our conversations and returned sure that not only is AIR here to stay, but it is gearing itself to remain the first choice for a radio listener. The next hundred years promise to be as exciting as the last hundred!

1

The Beginning

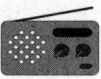

IT WAS THE MIDDLE OF JUNE 1984. IT HAD BEEN HARDLY A week from 8 June when the Indian Army had entered the Golden Temple in Amritsar to dislodge the Sikh militants holed up inside. The militants, who had amassed a colossal amount of weaponry inside, fired upon the army with machine guns and launched rockets at them from fortified positions in the Akal Takht, the temporal seat of the Sikh religion. The operation, titled 'Blue Star', left eighty-three army men dead and 239 injured. As per government figures, the total fatalities were 554. Over 1,500 militants were apprehended. Punjab was in turmoil and Sikhs worldwide protested this intrusion into their temporal space. As a result, many deserted the army and riots erupted all over the state, where a curfew was declared.

In this mayhem, when most did not even dare to leave their homes, Sukhjinder Kaur reached the gates of the Golden Temple and asked to be let in. A tall, strikingly good-looking Sikh woman in her late thirties, she was a producer at the AIR station in Jalandhar. That day, she had driven eighty kilometres to the Golden Temple, dodging roadblocks and risking her life, taking eight hours for a journey that would otherwise take less than two.

When the message that she and her station director wanted to enter the temple was sent to the brigadier, the senior-most army officer inside, he instantly refused. 'This is no place for a civilian to be right now,' he said, 'least of all a woman.'

Sukhjinder Kaur's answer to this rebuff is the stuff history is made of.

'Tell the brigadier sahab,' she said, 'it is not a woman asking to enter the premises—it is an officer of AIR.' She was instantly let in. She not only saw first-hand what had happened inside but recorded a programme based on interviews of civilians she interacted with outside the temple and broadcast it the following day.

It is a tribute to her bravery and the respect attached to AIR that she was amongst the first civilians to be allowed inside the premises after the military operation. It is such innumerable, dedicated professionals like her who have built the edifice that, despite the onslaught of television, OTT platforms, private radio stations and the internet, continues to command a listenership of tens of millions.

The radio, the medium Sukhjinder worked for, is an invention that is more than a century old.

Ask any school-going child about who invented the radio: the immediate answer would be Marconi. Guglielmo Marconi was an Italian scientist who got the Nobel Prize for physics in 1909 (which he shared with Karl Ferdinand Braun) for his contribution to developing wireless telegraphy. He is said to have confessed in his acceptance speech that he did not know how his invention worked.

When we ask her about Marconi, Sarita, a physics teacher, explains, 'This could probably be true because Marconi put the concept together, but the same was based on the work of many others.' Besides Braun, he also relied for his 'invention' on the work of Reginald Fessenden, who, it is said, first broadcast the human voice over radio in 1900. Marconi is also believed to have been inspired by the work of Heinrich Hertz, who had done a lot of work in the field of wireless transmission. Marconi replicated Hertz's experiments and sent a wireless message from the attic of his home to the basement. This so fascinated him that he decided to pursue this to make wireless transmission popular, seeing a lot of commercial possibilities in it. He also used the work of Sir Jagadish Chandra Bose, who had worked extensively in radio transmission but did not patent his inventions, which Marconi was prompt in doing.

'Marconi patented the radio, but when he could not exploit it commercially in Italy, he migrated to England and set up the Wireless Telegraph & Signal Company in 1897,' she adds. 'It broadcast its first radio programme from Chelmsford on 23 February 1920.'

We look at the history of radio in India and find that India was quick to follow this lead. For example, in collaboration with the Post and Telegraph department, we discover that *The Times of India* broadcast a musical programme from Bombay in November 1922. Sir George Lloyd, the then governor of Bombay Province, heard this programme in Pune.

Taking a cue from this event, radio broadcasting started in India with the Radio Club of Bombay in June 1923, followed by the Calcutta Radio Club in the same year and the Madras Radio Club a year later.

'A name that stands out in this effort is that of Krishnaswamy Chetty,' D.S. Arvind Chettiar, a young fourth-generation radio buff from the same family, tells us proudly.

'He was fascinated by the concept of being able to speak at one place and getting many to hear it at another,' he continued. 'So, after completing his education, he returned from England and brought a 20-watt radio transmitter with him. He set it up in our ancestral home in Madras and broadcast classical Carnatic music and devotional songs every day for three hours. He persuaded a select band of friends and relatives to buy radio sets and listen to the programme.'

'Those were the days when those who owned radio sets placed them in their houses where they would be visible to even those passing by, and played them at the topmost volume,' adds Swathi, his techie wife.

'My father told me there were often complaints to the police that the area's peace was being disturbed by those owning radios,' Arvind laughs aloud, recalling the conversation.

These radio buffs set up and ran the radio clubs purely on the strength of their passion. The government, on its part, aided the clubs by giving them a share of the revenue from licensing receiver sets. Unfortunately, though the programmes were immensely popular amongst the elite, the number of receivers was so small that the income was insufficient to fund the activity. Predictably, the three clubs went bankrupt within a matter of years.

Interestingly, when it closed, the Madras Radio Club gifted its transmitters to the Madras Municipal Corporation, which installed loudspeakers in the municipal garden and broadcast programmes for a few hours every evening.

The government then held detailed discussions with private parties on broadcasting as a viable business model and in 1926, the Indian Broadcasting Company (IBC) was formed. The major shareholders of this company were Raja Saheb Dhanraj Girji Narsingh Girji, the owner of Dhanraj Mills, who contributed 44 per cent of the ₹6 lakh subscribed capital, and the Indian Telegraph Company (owned in turn by the Marconi Company), which held another 43 per cent. Individual small shareholders had the rest.

The company started broadcasting from Bombay on 23 July 1927 and set up a station in Calcutta soon after. Revenue came from the 80 per cent share of the license fee and a 10 per cent cess on importing radio sets, and totalled ₹24,000 a month. The monthly expense was a staggering ₹33,000, and a large part of it went into salaries for the predominantly British senior staffers who were inducted primarily from the British Broadcasting Corporation (BBC). This capital was quickly exhausted as almost ₹4.5 lakh went into setting up the stations in Calcutta and Bombay and the rest subsidized the operations. The loss was financed mainly by mortgaging assets.

The company was perennially in the red and at the end of 1929, faced a loss of ₹3.82 lakh. Its ex-BBC staffers had also left by then. They had written a memorandum to the company in 1928 asking for higher salaries, demanding an astronomical amount of 2,000 pounds sterling for the general manager and proportionate amounts for all the others. They were promptly shipped back. Many Indian advisors also quit the company, complaining about the neglect of Indian sentiment while choosing what to broadcast. This initial effort to create a radio network in India ended with the company voluntarily liquidating itself on 1 March 1930.

Predictably, there was a hue and cry. The elite and the existing license holders protested because they were denied their exclusive pleasure and their licenses became defunct. However, dealers in radio sets were the most vociferous in their demand to continue radio broadcasts.

'My grandfather told me we almost went bankrupt that year,' says Rahul Madan, owner of the Oriental Radio and Electric Company. He has two outlets in Daryagunj and Karol Bagh in Delhi, the first of which was started in 1929. It stocked radio sets and radiograms from Telefunken, the German company.

He adds, 'We had stock worth more than a lakh of rupees back then, which we had imported in the hope of radio catching on in a big way, and we stood to lose it all. Not only this, there was a sizeable repair economy and all those families would have been on the roads.'

'Yes, mine was such a family,' says Dinesh Kamat from old Goa. 'My father and grandfather ran radio repair shops then and it was a flourishing business.' He laughs aloud as he recounts how customers would come to his father's shop lugging bulky radio sets. 'The sets worked on valves in those days and the valves would have algae growing on them if the sets were not switched on regularly, particularly in the Goan monsoons. So, all my father would do is open the rear panel and use a room heater to dry out the insides and the set would be as good as new the next morning!'

He explains that the elite abandoned the older ones as manufacturers and importers introduced newer models. The mechanics then repaired and sold these to buffs who could not afford the latest sets, priced above ₹500, a considerable sum those days. As a result of the shutdown, this sizeable force of radio mechanics also stood to lose their livelihood.

They all pressured the government through local politicians and it decided to take over the operation of the bankrupt Indian Broadcasting Company. Thus, in 1931, the Indian State Broadcasting Service (ISBS) was born, which, at a written-down cost, took over the bankrupt company's assets and decided to run it for two years on an experimental basis.

One of the first recruits to this corporation was Lionel Fielden, who joined the ISBS from the BBC as the controller of broadcasting. Though recruited by the ISBS, he was responsible for changing its name to the current one.

Not happy with the existing name (he considered it too bureaucratic), he mentioned it to the then viceroy Lord Linlithgow at a banquet.

'Yes, quite a mouthful, isn't it?' commented the viceroy.

'Exactly, Your Excellency,' concurred Fielden. 'We need something that conveys that radio will soon be broadcast all over India. Something simpler, easier on the tongue.'

'How about All India Radio,' said the viceroy, rising to the bait. 'The very thing!' exclaimed Fielden, 'what beautiful initials!' Thus, in 1936, the name was changed to All India Radio.

It was called Akashvani in Hindi and the name continues to be used to date. There are many versions of how the word was coined, the most prevalent being the one attributed to Nobel Laureate Rabindranath Tagore. In 1938, at the inauguration of Calcutta AIR's shortwave transmission service, Tagore dedicated a poem to it called 'Akashvani'. The poem, which inspired the name, read:

>   Hark to Akashvani upsurging
>   From here below,
>   The earth is bathed in Heaven's glory
>   Its purple glow,
>   Across the blue expanse is firmly planted
>   The altar of the Muse;
>   The lyre unheard of Light is throbbing
>   With human hues,
>   From earth to heaven, distance conquered
>   In waves of light,
>   Flows the music of man's divining
>   Fancy's flight,
>   To East and West speech careers,
>   Swift as the Sun,
>   The mind of man reaches Heaven's confines,
>   Its freedom won …

Another version lies in the claim made by Anuradhagiri Rao, who said, as per an article in *The New Indian Express* in 2012, that her father, late Hosbet Rama Rao, had first coined the word in a booklet he had published in 1932. The fifteen–twenty-page booklet explained what radio was, and was widely read and appreciated by the literate classes. In this booklet, the word 'Akashvani' was first used to refer to radio.

According to the report, she claimed that Rama Rao drew inspiration from a mythological tale in the Bhagvata Purana, in which Kansa heard a voice predicting his death at the hands of his sister Devaki's eighth child. It was, literally, a voice ('vani') from the skies ('akash'), hence the coining of the term.

In another version, while celebrating the diamond jubilee of the first radio broadcast, AIR, Mysore officially credited Prof. M.V. Gopalaswamy, who taught psychology at Mysore University, for coining the word in 1935. But here, too, the more exciting version gives credit to his wife.

As the story goes, Gopalaswamy, a radio buff with diverse interests, decided to set up a radio station at his Bangalore residence. But, with the transmitter in place and broadcasts about to begin, he was stuck for a proper name that would convey the exact meaning. As he and his radio mechanic friend Jagadish wrestled with the problem, his wife Kamala Pati overheard all this while she was cooking, and walked over to ask what was being named.

'It is a new device through which voices will travel through the air and be heard elsewhere,' explained Prof. Gopalaswamy, using the words 'Akasha' (sky) and 'Vani' (for sound).

'Ahha, Akashvani!' she said, and an iconic word was coined.

The newly set up ISBS looked at the revenues and found that the number of licenses had decreased marginally during the previous year from 7,775 to 7,719. Therefore, after analysing the prospects of an immediate increase in revenue and finding it minimal, it decided to cut down the expenses and reduce them from ₹33,000 to ₹22,000.

'This resulted in losses halting,' says Deepankar Majumdar, a retired station director from AIR, 'but when the world over expenses on broadcasting were being increased to offer better programming, we were reducing them.'

The cost-cutting did not help and in 1931, exactly a year and six months after having taken over broadcasting, and considering that the economy was in a state of extreme depression, the government decided to stop broadcasting.

'We were on the road again,' says Madan, 'With more stock than before. Not only that, but the government specifically stated that it knew dealers would lose money, but in the national interest, it did not see any options. This time, we knew all was lost.'

All, however, was not lost. On the contrary, protests erupted on a large scale, particularly in Calcutta. Yielding to them, on 5 May 1932, the government announced that it was increasing the customs duty on imported receiver sets from 12.5 per cent to 50 per cent and continuing with the service. Since then, closing down transmission was never again discussed and broadcasting remained firmly under governmental control.

The year 1933 was good for the ISBS. The number of licensed radio receivers increased to 10,785, which, along with a rise in customs duties, ensured that the ISBS ended up with a surplus of ₹2.7 lakh. The steady rise continued and the number of sets increased to 2,47,421 at Independence in 1947.

We ask Madan about how his family business fared during the period.

'Good money was made from sales of new sets, but we made more in a side hustle,' he chuckles as he responds. Apparently, most shops offered exchange bonuses for bringing in old sets while buying new ones, then repairing the old sets and selling them in the gray market. This income, as per Madan, was much more than that from selling new sets.

We ask him if his grandfather also made his fortune through such sets and he winks and asks us if we want coffee!

There was a massive revenue leakage with the gray market sets not paying any license fee. The government took serious note of this and employed a number of inspectors to conduct raids and unearth unlicensed sets. This practice was given so much importance even after Independence that 'detector vans' used for this purpose were given pride of place along with the Police and Fire Brigade in the Republic Day parades.

'When I was about ten years old, my father brought me what was then called a crystal set,' says Vandan Paranjpe, an English teacher in her sixties whose father had worked for AIR. 'It was a small device that could only pick the local radio station and be heard over headphones as it had no speakers and did not require a license to own. However, one day, my mother got into an argument with a neighbour who complained to the postal department that we owned an unlicensed radio set.'

Vandan tells us there was a raid at her house within a week and the inspector insisted on checking their small flat to locate the set. However, the raid was called off after showing him the crystal set and her father explaining that he worked for AIR and would never do something to harm its interests.

'I hid under the table, thinking the police would take me away,' she concludes with a giggle.

She shows us an old radio license, a passport-sized document with a dark blue cover and the printed radio emblem. Inside, it has license fee stamps, much like postal stamps, with the seal of the post office and a few signatures scribbled over them. Renewed annually, the value of the stamps were ₹3 every year, rising to ₹15 from 1981 to 1990. However, the cost of collection was always higher than the revenue; the license fee was finally abolished as late as 1991.

The terms and conditions of the license make for interesting reading. The set was for use only by the licensee and his family on its licensed premises. Any changes were to be informed to the licensing authorities. The license was to be transferred to the new buyer if the set was sold. It could be impounded if these were disregarded or the set was placed in a commercial building.

In 1935, the government was pleased with broadcasting delivering a surplus and took the job seriously. Soon, a new radio station in Delhi was set up, which would also be its headquarters in the years to come.

In her book *Connaught Place and the Making of New Delhi*, Dr Swapna Liddle, a noted historian, has this to say about the location of Broadcasting House on what is now called Parliament Street:

> Interestingly, it was called Parliament Street even in the 1920s, though the building after which it was named, was still called Council House. The important road was to witness the construction of several institutional buildings. The Imperial Bank of India opened a branch here on 1 January1926, and Reuters moved into the new building on this road in 1928. ... Broadcasting House, housing the studios of All India Radio, was built in 1943.

The Reuters building was rebuilt and now houses the offices of the Press Trust of India, whereas the Imperial Bank building currently houses the Reserve Bank of India and has been substantially renovated. The only building to stand majestically is the red brick-faced building of the Broadcasting House.

'Have you noticed the shape of the building?' asks Obaid Niazi, a retired producer from AIR, when we meet him over coffee at the Press Club of India. Then, noticing our bewilderment, he chuckles and explains, 'It is shaped exactly like the spool deck on which the tapes used to be run for broadcast in those times. The two circular portions on the sides are the spools and the central circular portion is the tape head.' We realize we had never noticed this. Walking over to Parliament Street, we stand across the road near the gates of the Reserve Bank of India and take in the majesty of the building.

The Calcutta and Bombay lobbies strongly resisted the headquarters' move to Delhi, citing that spotting and nurturing talent in these places was easier. Delhi's scorching summer was another reason and the cost of moving all broadcasting to Shimla, where the government moved in the summers, was considered prohibitive.

However, Delhi was the national capital, which overrode every other logic, and the shift was completed, with the offices accommodated in various rented buildings in and around Connaught Place. The basement of a bungalow on Alipore Road was converted into the first studio in 1936.

'Most broadcasts in that period were live,' says J. Nagarajan, ex-administrator of the Sant Paramanand Charitable Eye Hospital, the building that now occupies the site. 'Whereas it was possible to broadcast most programmes from the studios, they were too small to accommodate the military bands that performed for radio regularly, which then played from the front lawns. Moreover, the noise of cars and tongas moving on the road often wove into the broadcasts. Hence, a man was specially employed to stand on the road and stop the traffic when broadcasts were on,' he informs us, delivering an interesting aside.

He shows us a plaque marking the studio's location in the hospital's basement. As we thank him and leave, we notice that the spot marked is right next to the department of radiodiagnosis and we smile at each other at the association of the word radio as we exit the building.

The offices and studios shifted to the Broadcasting House in May 1943 and have remained on the premises ever since.

A vital decision was taken between the late thirties and early forties, which helped cultivate the radio listening habit among the Indian populace. This decision was about the choice of technology, and therein lies a tale.

In 1935, a senior official from the research department of BBC, Mr H.L. Kirke, was sent to India to prepare a report on utilizing the ₹40 lakh allotted for setting up new stations. He toured the country along with Fielden and prepared a report recommending setting up large-capacity mediumwave transmitters in various cities.

However, Mr C.W. Goyder, also from the BBC, who took over as chief engineer in 1936, disagreed. He felt that the mediumwave transmitters would cover a tiny percentage of the country and recommended setting up a few shortwave transmitters instead. He believed these, supplemented by existing mediumwave transmitters, would serve a more significant percentage of the population at a fraction of the cost.

'How does a shortwave transmission score over mediumwave transmission?' we ask Obaid Niazi.

'A mediumwave transmitter delivers higher fidelity over a smaller area,' he explains, 'whereas a shortwave transmitter delivers essentially as second-rate quality but covers a larger area and costs much less. It is like the argument about concrete roads versus tar roads, wherein concrete roads cost more and connect a smaller area. In contrast, tar roads connect more but deliver comparatively poorer though acceptable quality.'

Goyder's opinion was accepted and shortwave stations were set up in the four metros in the late 1930s. Each covered an area of almost 800 km around the metro and provided two channels for broadcast. This freed up space so that two sets of programmes (for Indians and Europeans) could be broadcast simultaneously. This also made interlinking between stations possible so that one station could relay the programme of another, adding variety to the broadcasts.

Due to the availability of bandwidth, Indian programming increased. For example, the Bombay station started broadcasting a rural interest programme in Marathi, Gujarati and Kannada, a lead that the other stations soon followed. This expanded the listener base substantially, leading to greater interest in setting up more radio stations.

Broadcasting also caught the fancy of the Indian princely states and a few of them started their own radio stations. Mysore already had a station set up by Prof. Gopalaswamy called Akashvani. However, it lost money despite a grant from the Municipal Committee and the Mysore state took it over in 1942.

The nizam of Hyderabad set up two radio stations in Hyderabad and Aurangabad in 1935 and the states of Gwalior, Baroda and Travancore followed.

The setting up of shortwave stations, as per the recommendations of Goyder, cost only five and a half lakh rupees and released a substantial amount from the allocated budget for setting up stations at newer locations. As a result, at the time of Independence in 1947, British India had nine operating radio stations. Lahore, Dacca and Peshawar went to Pakistan, while Calcutta, Lucknow, Delhi, Bombay, Madras and Tiruchirappalli stayed with India. The broadcasting stations from the princely states also merged into AIR when they acceded to the India Union, giving it a footprint across India, which has since increased exponentially to enter every home in the country.

During this period, many households had more than one radio set and fans cultivated the hobby of collecting sets from the world over. We meet Hardeep Singh Chandpuri, an energetic, soft-spoken, pleasant man in his early fifties who dons many hats. He is a radio jockey, a publisher and runs an academy for training broadcast professionals. He shows us his collection of twenty-two radio sets, with the oldest going back seventy-plus years. There is a radio in a briefcase, a pure white American model never introduced in India and one shaped like a cathedral, among many others.

'My grandfather started the collection in the early 1940s,' he tells us, 'and I am forever looking at adding to it.'

The '40s were a period when everyone was in love with the radio, which is unsurprising. Even all the prominent Indian leaders, despite their opposition to most things British, took a keen interest in and expressed appreciation of AIR.

At the behest of Jawaharlal Nehru, Mumbai station started a children's programme. When he visited it in 1936, he wrote words of appreciation in the visitor's book, as did Sarojini Naidu when she visited in 1934. She commented, 'To harness the ether for those who dwell upon the earth is one of the loveliest services that the modern age can render to humanity–Upward Radio!' Another person of note who visited AIR studios was C. Rajagopalachari, who spoke at the inauguration of the Madras radio station.

'Do I have to speak into this?' Mahatma Gandhi had asked, pointing to the microphone. He had stepped into the studios of the Columbia Broadcasting Service from Kingsley Hall for his first-ever broadcast. Gandhi was then in London to attend the Second Round Table Conference (on the constitutional progress of India) in September 1931. He made an impassioned plea for Independence while addressing the listeners from America to whom the station catered.

He had said, 'If India is to perpetuate the glory of her ancient past, it can do so only when it attains freedom. The reason for the struggle having drawn the attention of the world, I know, does not lie in the fact that we Indians are fighting for our liberty, but in the fact that the means adopted by us for attaining that liberty are unique and, as far as history shows us, have not been adopted by any other people of whom we have any record.'

He ended the speech by saying, 'May I not, then, on behalf of these semi-starved millions, appeal to the conscience of the world to come to the rescue of a people dying for regaining its liberty?'

The canny politician that he was, he used the power of radio to appeal to a vast international audience!

But Gandhi knew that a tiny population in India accessed the radio and never used it to reach the masses. It may sound strange today, but he realized that the power of public speeches, covered by newspapers and read all over India, was far superior to radio speeches.

He spoke for the second time (his first and only time on AIR) on 14 November 1947. He wanted to visit the refugees who were camped at Kurukshetra after fleeing Pakistan in the aftermath of the violent Partition. However, being advised not to travel for security reasons, he addressed them through radio. The day is now commemorated as 'Public Service Broadcasting Day'.

Barely two and a half months after that, he was shot dead by Nathuram Godse at Birla House in Delhi. The radio, which Gandhi never considered a medium to reach the masses, now conveyed the news of his death nationwide.

2

The Spoken Word: The News

THE TECHNICIAN IN CHARGE OF STUDIO NUMBER 5 WAS UNDER tremendous stress. He kept checking and rechecking the equipment but found nothing wrong with them. He had, after all, been doing this for days now. He could look at the console and instinctively understand what was wrong. He was sure nothing was wrong, yet the scheduled broadcast was not coming through. 'So is Gandhiji late today?' The thought crossed his mind, but he quickly brushed it aside because he knew this had never happened before—Gandhiji had never been late for a prayer meeting!

Studio 5 in Broadcasting House relayed Gandhiji's prayer meeting from Birla House every day and it started at 5 p.m. on the dot without exception. However, it was already fifteen minutes overdue and though the speakers were on and the system was operational, all he heard was the background noise of the crowd. Officers rushed in to find out what was wrong but could not detect anything. Then, as they peered intently into their consoles, waiting for the prayers to come through at 5.30 p.m., a time imprinted on the nation's memories forever, they heard three loud blasts in the background. It startled them, but they ignored the sound, assuming it to be crackers, and rechecked their machines when a panic-stricken voice shouted, 'Gandhiji *ko golee maar di* (Someone has shot Gandhiji).' An eerie silence descended on the studio as some people stood shell-shocked while others started running helter-skelter, not knowing how to react.

The news, though not made public, spread like wildfire in the streets of Delhi.

Dr Kelkar, dean of Music College at Vadodara, recalls what his father had told him, 'The local radio at Baroda continued to repeatedly play Gandhiji's favourite "*Vaishnava Jana To Tene Kahiye*", making people wonder what was going on. When Melville de Mellow came on air and said, "Please stand by for grave news," they realized something horrifying had happened.' De Mellow repeated this thrice before breaking the heart-wrenching news and the radio switched over to music for mourning. All those who had not heard it the first time stayed glued to their radio sets for the 6 p.m. news when it was reconfirmed. A pall of gloom descended on the nation as people took to the streets, wailing and crying, while those in Delhi rushed towards Birla House.

Melville's baritone captured the grief of an entire nation as he poignantly described the scenes unfolding in front of him.

'In the room, the scene was heartrending,' recalled de Mellow subsequently, in a sombre voice. 'The walls were white, the room was furnished ... but these blue carpets contrasted with the white mattress upon which lay Mahatmaji. Moreover, he was shrouded in spotless white khadi, from his feet to abdomen.' And then de Mellow's voice, steady thus far, softened as he began to describe the Mahatma's body. 'His chest was bare; I could see the dark patches of the assassin's bullets against the skin of his frail body. His eyes were closed; his face was a man's face in prayer.'

As de Mellow turned to leave, he saw Pandit Nehru enter and stand near him. De Mellow paused, his pain evident in the following line: 'Then he lowered his head and I saw a heartbroken Prime Minister weep.'

In the most significant news broadcast of post-Independent India, Nehru stood in the studios of AIR and delivered with a choked voice a speech as well-known as his 'Tryst with Destiny' speech on the eve of Independence.

'Friends and comrades, the light has gone out of our lives and there is darkness everywhere. I do not know what to tell you and how to say it. Our beloved leader, Bapu as we called him, the Father of the Nation, is no more,' said Nehru. AIR was a witness to the recording of history.

The country again switched on all its radio sets on 2 February when Melville de Mellow covered the funeral of Gandhiji, speaking for a total of seven hours with some minor breaks for the Hindi commentary.

An Anglo-Indian from Jodhpur, de Mellow worked for AIR until 1971. He produced and lent his deep, sonorous voice with the oh-so-perfect diction to many pathbreaking programmes. Whether it was reading the news, covering sports events, wars, Republic Day parades or swearings-in, there was no genre where de Mellow did not raise the bar and set new standards. He went on to become not only the best-known newscaster but probably the most renowned voice in the history of AIR.

The history of news broadcasts goes back to the early decades of the twentieth century. The first-ever news bulletin in the country was in English and went on air from the Bombay station on 23 July 1927, under the private Indian Broadcasting Company. Then, on 26 August 1927, IBC started a Bengali bulletin from the Calcutta station. When it went bankrupt in 1930 and the government took over broadcasting, it continued with the same pattern. Till 1935, one bulletin each in English and Hindustani were broadcast from Bombay and one in Bengali from Calcutta.

Just as the popularity of the elite game of cricket grew with the introduction of commentary in Hindi, the real growth in listenership of news broadcasts came after 1936, when the first bulletin in Hindi was aired from the newly started Delhi station. The Second World War gave a fillip to news broadcasts and a monitoring unit was also set up to track foreign broadcasts. By then, AIR was broadcasting current affairs programmes besides news bulletins in English, Hindi, some regional languages and a few foreign languages. Anecdotes abound of how news was aired then. The most interesting is how a cyclist carried it to the studios on Alipore Road after the news bulletin was prepared in the Broadcasting House on Parliament Street.

When the Lahore, Peshawar and Lucknow stations started operating, the news was relayed to them over phone lines and then aired. However, this transmission mode was too expensive and receiver stations were later installed at these locations to relay the news bulletins live from Delhi, over the shortwave.

AIR sourced content from Reuters and Associated Press of India, both London-based companies which had their Indian operations headquartered in Bombay. These news agencies had feet on the ground in India and arranged with many foreign news agencies for their input. They made news curated from all these sources available to AIR. Their fee was calculated using a slab-based formula linked to the number of radio licences issued. The same system continued post-Independence when agreements were signed with the Press Trust of India and United News of India to provide content.

The '50s till the advent of television in the '70s was, undoubtedly, the golden age of newscasting on AIR. Superstars like Pearson Surita, Surajit Sen, Dicky Rutnagur, Latika Ratnam, Barun Haldar, Roshan Menon and Sushil Jhaveri graced the English news unit. At the same time, Devki Nandan Pandey, Ashok Vajpayee, Vinod Kashyap and others lit up the Hindi newsroom. In addition, there was the phalanx of regional stars, as revered in their states as the big names were known nationally.

We spend hours in the AIR Archives listening to these golden voices enthralling the nation and realize that each has a different and unique style.

To learn more about these broadcasting stars, we sit with Manoj Atreya, a production executive with the central production unit who has had a long innings with AIR, moving through different departments and currently producing a clutch of magazine programmes. A middle-aged man with a slim frame that belies his age and experience, and a deep, resonant voice that can shift effortlessly between Hindi, English and Urdu, he is a trade veteran with thirty-three years of experience in broadcasting. His diction and pronunciation are impeccable and many current stars in the broadcast world consider him their inspiration. We quiz him about his learnings from the greats.

'Each one had their strong points,' says Manoj, 'but they were all sticklers for correct pronunciation, and the stories about their insistence on getting a word right are legion.'

He tells us about Sushil Jhaveri and says that in 1980, when Prakash Padukone was likely to win the All England Badminton Championships, Sushil got the Indian star to record the correct way of articulating his surname.

'Getting it wrong would have been a sin for him!' Manoj emphasizes by banging his palm on his working table, demonstrating that the passion for correctly using the language was alive and kicking in him.

'I have seen Barun Haldar personally ring up the embassies or consulates of countries of dignitaries expected to visit India and get the correct pronunciations of their names. Also, Barun Da religiously maintained a pigeonhole in the newsroom, where he kept cue cards with the correct pronunciations of words written down and alphabetically arranged.'

We ask Manoj if he has ever heard of rivalry between the newscasters and he replies in the negative. 'As a matter of fact, there was great respect,' he tells us. He quotes from an interview in which Haldar called de Mellow the 'best newscaster in the world', Menon the 'best in India' and Pandey the 'best reader of Hindi news'.

We bemoan that we cannot meet either since Haldar passed on in Kolkata in 2019 and Jhaveri succumbed to COVID-19 in 2020.

We carry this conversation to the tastefully decorated office of Sunit Tandon, an eminent radio personality and currently the director (programmes) of the India Habitat Centre. Tall, slim and dapperly dressed, he offers us lemon tea and takes forward the conversation about the greats of newscasting and his experience of working with them.

'It was not just about pronunciation either. It was also about the correct framing of a sentence,' continues Tandon. 'Even if a news item was handed to Barun Da as he entered the studio, he would give a quizzical look, take his pen, underline it for the correct pauses and check for grammar and spelling, even as he switched the microphone on—all in one go!'

'Amongst the newsreaders, Surajit Sen had undoubtedly the most resounding bass voice, deeper even than Melville de Mellow's baritone,' adds Tandon, talking about another great. 'He was the chief newsreader when I first started reading AIR's news as a casual artiste and all of us neophytes used to be his fans. Behind this extraordinary voice were intelligence, wit and a sense of humour that were very endearing. He could be pretty irreverent off the air,' chuckles Tandon. He recalls Sen sometimes even putting down the fader in the middle of a bulletin, to switch off the mic temporarily and let out an off-the-cuff remark about an annoying news item. 'This was for the sole benefit of anybody who happened to be in the studio with him!' recalls Tandon. He gives an example of a comment on a political figure that makes us roar with laughter, though he makes us commit that we will not name the personality or the comment while writing about this.

'Most of us are familiar with the iconic black and white photograph of 16 December 1971, showing General A.A.K. Niazi and General Jagjit Singh Aurora seated at a table, signing the Document of Surrender that led to the Independence of Bangladesh. However, few know that the person kneeling on the ground and holding a microphone recording the event for posterity is Surajit Sen,' Tandon enlightens us. He tells us that Surajit also covered the massacre of Israeli athletes during the Munich Olympics. Legend has it that he was present on the spot, recorded the event and scribbled the headline on a piece of paper while hiding in a ditch!

Usha Joshi, a retired newscaster from the Marathi news unit, talks about Ramanuj Prasad Singh, the legendary Hindi newsreader. 'He was so popular that he would use his initials while travelling by train. If the full name appeared on the list, people would seek him out, wondering if he was the same person they had heard on the radio. His wife, Manimala Singh, served as a newsreader in the Nepali service of AIR and he often used to joke that it was because of his deep voice that she married him.'

To explore the golden age of Indian newscasting, we look for a newscaster who has seen it all. The search leads us to Deepak Dholakia, who was in charge of the Gujarati news unit in AIR for nearly three decades.

Curious about what happened behind the scenes, we ask him how the News Services Division worked in his time.

'Two language units shared a room,' he tells us. 'Each unit had to broadcast three bulletins daily except for the Hindi and English units, which had hourly bulletins. We worked in shifts, each consisting of four to five newsreader-translators. First, the news feed from the agencies and the correspondents came into the general newsroom. Next, the editorial staff marked the national and international headlines, got them typed, cyclostyled and sent to regional units. In addition, state-specific items were then sent to the respective language units. Each bulletin would thus be a mix of national and international news items and a few pieces about the respective state. The team of newsreader-translators would then translate them into their respective languages. Finally, accompanied by a stand-by, one would take the bulletin to the studio to be read.'

He also tells us that these bulletins broadcast by the Delhi station were referred to as national bulletins despite the inclusion of some regional news items. The local news units in the respective states aired the regional news, which had only a passing reference to national and international events.

When we express our appreciation of the emphasis newsreaders placed on correct pronunciation and diction, Dholakia tells us that this had become a part of the culture of AIR because of the direction set by the greats. He informs us that this was institutionalized in the '60s when the then director of news, J.C. Mathur, set up a pronunciation cell in the division. He also started recording four bulletins randomly chosen every month for each newsreader, which the cell checked for correctness. The mistakes were mentioned in the 'annual confidential report' of the newsreader concerned and affected their career. This made everybody wary of making even the slightest of errors.

'We exchanged information freely,' says Milind Deshpande, a newscaster with over thirty years of experience. 'For example, when the Tamil Nadu politician Kanimozhi first got elected to Parliament, we rushed to the Tamil unit to learn how to pronounce her name. Once, two senior newsreaders from the English unit walked into the Marathi unit arguing about how the words Gudhi Padwa, the festival of the Marathi new year, was pronounced. One insisted "Padwa" had a "d" sound in it, while the other was vehement that it had "dh" and neither would take the bulletin on air till it was settled,' says he.

Deshpande is probably one of the few who had initially worked with cyclostyled news bulletins and now works with the latest state-of-the-art equipment for creating bulletins. He is energetic, almost sixty years old and due to retire in 2022. He seems like the right 'go-to' person to answer any questions about the transition from the 'ticker tape and cyclostyling' times to the computer age, and we make a mental note to see him again.

Because of this dedication, the newscasters were held as gold standards in how a language was spoken. Parents would often ask children to listen to the news to correct their diction and improve their vocabulary. Even aspirants for the civil services were advised by their coaches to learn to speak like the newsreaders to clear their interview rounds. Therefore, the superstar status accorded to newsreaders then comes as no surprise.

This was brought home to us when we visited Jyoti Deshpande, a ninety-year-old ex-employee of the old Portuguese administration of Goa, for an interview for another story we are doing on the liberation of Goa.

We had been forewarned that she was wary of strangers and would not readily agree to meet us. The warning was prophetic and her maid refused to open the door for us or even listen to us until we mentioned that maybe she knew Neelesh's father, Datta Kulkarni, a newscaster on AIR. In just under a minute, she let us in. His name had literally opened the door for us.

'I grew up hearing the news read by him,' she said excitedly, as she bid us to sit down and asked the maid to get us tea. 'You want to hear me mimic him?' she asked shyly, mimicking the opening announcement as read by Neelesh's father. We laughed out loud: the ice was broken.

While sitting with Dr Atul K. Tiwary, ex-additional director-general, News Services Division, we recount the incident. He is not surprised at hearing our Goa story and is quick to explain why.

'For the regular radio news listeners, the newsreader is like a family friend,' he says. 'Not only are they familiar with the newsreader's voice after hearing it year after year, but they have also learnt to trust it. The subliminal association of radio news with reliability gets transferred in their minds to the newsreader, too. So, the person she was welcoming was a close and trusted family friend's son.'

Dr Tiwary, who was in charge of the AIR General News Room, is someone who, in his own words, 'studied medicine to please his father and took the civil services entrance to please his mother and made it through both.' He is pleasant and open and a Fulbright scholar whose youthful looks belie his mid-fifties age and extensive experience, including stints in the Prime Minister's office media cell and a posting as a foreign correspondent of AIR before seeking voluntary retirement for pursuing other interests.

'Our mantra for newscasting can be summed up with the first three letters of the alphabet,' explains Dr Tiwary. 'We strive for Accuracy, Brevity and Clarity. Our core listeners are students, senior citizens, housewives, journalists, diplomats and policymakers, and they very much appreciate this.'

He emphasizes that reliability is the core USP of the news on AIR and is something they take great pains to ensure. 'That is what differentiates us from news channels anywhere else. We don't speculate, we don't guess and we don't make anything up! We get facts, verify them and only then broadcast them. So, we always emphasize ensuring that anything that goes out of our studios is 100 per cent correct.'

Samir Kumar, former head of Prasar Bharati News Service (PBNS) and Digital Platform (DP), the news agency Prasar Bharati was building in-house, agrees. 'We checked every bit of information multiple times. We were fully aware that, as Prasar Bharati, we represent India, so everything we say is accepted as the country's stand. We couldn't afford to be wrong,' says Samir.

He gives an example of how an intern in his tenure had used the word 'boycott' for India's non-participation in the Winter Olympics in China. There was an intense discussion about whether to use the word boycott. Samir says he then sent the entire news item to a secretary in the external affairs ministry from where the news item originated and, within twenty minutes, got a response on what the correct usage should be; only then was the item released.

'The word boycott has a specific meaning in diplomacy,' says Samir. 'Hence, using the wrong word could have embarrassed the government and the ministry from which the news emanated. If the choice is between being a bit late but correct, and verified and quick but not 100 per cent sure, we choose the former, always!'

We decided to go into PBNS and DP, the sterling work done by the organization and its abrupt closure later and turn to more stories on the accuracy of news items broadcast by AIR.

Milind Deshpande cites an example of the necessity of verifying information before putting it on the air.

'I was on duty when three bomb blasts shook Mumbai in 1993. We had private television channels blaring out the news, showing gory visuals and going ballistic about how a fourth blast had also occurred and speculating on where the fifth one would happen. I was the shift in charge on duty and rushed to the newsroom asking permission to include the item in the next news bulletin, due in a few minutes. But, till that time, the AIR correspondent on the ground in Mumbai had not confirmed the news and my request was flatly turned down. It was frustrating but that was necessary. It was brought home to us in just a few minutes when our correspondent called to say there had been only three blasts. When we said there were three explosions, all the television channels changed tack and started saying the same. What was astonishing was that none of the channels that aired the incorrect item bothered to apologize for spreading misinformation on an issue involving public order. Had

AIR done this, heads would have rolled and the same channels would have gone on and on about our callousness,' he concludes.

The News Services Division, NSD, now operates from the New Broadcasting House, just behind the iconic AIR building on Parliament Street. The Delhi station handles the national news and broadcasts 607 bulletins in ninety-two languages from the central and regional news units (RNU). In addition, it broadcasts numerous current affairs programmes on a wide variety of topics. There are political and social discussions called *Spotlight*, *Parikrama*, *Surkhiyon Mein*, *Aaj Savere* and others besides the *Sports Scan* and *Money Talk*. A top-rated programme is *Market Mantra*, which features news from the stock markets and is widely heard and trusted. In addition, the news is uploaded to the News Services Division website, www.newsonair.com, Facebook, X (formerly Twitter) and YouTube. Its website garners over one million page views per month. The X handle has 3.3 million followers, while the YouTube channel has 6,75,000 subscribers, as of 2024. The regional news units headquartered in state capitals and some important cities of the respective states also have their own social media presence.

In the seventy-fifth year of Independence, many special programmes on nationalistic themes were being put on the air by NSD. These included a programme called *Dharohar*, which had broadcasts of speeches from leaders of the freedom movement taken from the archives, a programme on unsung heroes of the freedom struggle called *Veergatha* and another featuring patriotic songs from that era titled *Azadi ke Tarane*. The Amrit Mahotsav quiz was also aired on the news daily to engage younger audiences. Simple questions about the fight for Independence were asked in every bulletin and answers were solicited on WhatsApp and email. The questions were deliberately kept simple to increase engagement and almost ten thousand responses were received daily and the winners were chosen by lottery. The day's winner got to record a thirty-second sound bite broadcast the next day and the postal department delivered a small token gift home, free of charge.

Dr Tiwary makes a few phone calls and gets us permission to visit the general newsroom, whose operations he was directly responsible for while posted as ADG and provides the content for all the national bulletins. He takes us around the newsrooms, of which there are two—the Hindi and the general newsroom.

The GNR, as it is referred to, is crackling with action. It is a far cry from the newsroom that Deepak Dholakia had described, wherein teleprinters spewed out rolls upon rolls of paper bearing all kinds of news items and staffers rushed them to various desks inhabited by the editorial staff. In that era, the sub and assistant editors discarded a few, cut and pruned others and sent them off either to the chief news editor for the national news or to the regional desks for onward transmission to the regional news units. Instead, the general newsroom is now like any corporate office where people quietly sit and work on computer screens. The running frenzy we expected in a newsroom is nowhere visible. However, the editor-in-charge (the ENS) on duty seems agitated and is gesturing urgently to someone, waving a piece of paper. Dr Tiwary explains that the newsreader had already entered the studio for the afternoon bulletin and the ENS had received an item he felt had to be added. The urgency was to ensure it got to the studios in time.

'What will he do now?' we ask Deepa Sahni, a mid-forties Indian Information Services officer. As the ENS is busy with the bulletin, Dr Tiwary has asked Deepa, the editor on duty, to take us around the newsroom.

'This will be put on the storyboard and rushed to the studio. The item will get to the studio almost a minute before the newscasts start and that's enough time to adjust the headlines,' Deepa says.

'What if this had happened a minute later when the bulletin was already on the air?' we ask her.

'Normally, the editor who has prepared the bulletin is on standby in the studio. A normal ten-minute bulletin consists of 140 lines typed in double space, so she has enough space to edit the rest of the news bulletin and prepare a new storyboard for the newsreader. If she finds that deleting anything is impossible, the newsreader will either increase the delivery speed or drop the repetition of the headline at the end to accommodate this. Of course, this is on the presumption that we have two or three minutes for the bulletin to end. If something comes in with just a minute or two to spare, it is held back for the next bulletin unless it is some major event.' Deepa informs us that the decision on inclusion always rests with the editor in the studio, who decides on the spot and whose word is final.

Our friend Milind Deshpande, who worked in the GNR just before retirement, explains how a bulletin is prepared.

'News items coming in from all our sources on the system are picked up if found newsworthy and edited and put into the general pool by the pool desk—a continuous process supervised by the ENS. Then, the regional desk picks up the items of interest to the respective states, curates them along with the national news items and puts them on the system for that particular state or region. The regional news units, in turn, add to this the district- and city-level items they receive, and prepare their bulletins. There is also a reverse flow by which items that the regional news units consider of national importance are sent to the regional desk in Delhi. The language desk does a similar job for the foreign languages heard in neighbouring countries. Finally, the national bulletin, the main activity of the NSD Delhi office, is prepared by the compiling desk, which picks up items from the pool and curates them. Simultaneously, other staffers work on the items to be uploaded to social media and others curate items for the various magazine programmes,' he concludes.

We walk with Deepa into the control room of studio number 1 to see first-hand how the news is read out. The newsreader is at the microphone and a standby newsreader and the editor who compiled the news bulletin are with him. He carries the storyboard with him and reads from it. Suddenly the studio door opens and a person rushes in with a slip of paper. There is a flurry of activity as the editor flips through the stacked pages of the storyboard, scribbles a correction on one of them and passes it on to the newsreader, who calmly continues reading without batting an eyelid. We now realize that what had seemed a simple exercise when we heard about it from Deepa Sahni, requires tremendous coordination and extreme presence of mind. We wonder why it couldn't be done using software and the teleprompter.

'Our newsreaders are not comfortable using the teleprompter and since they are managing it so well, we have no reason to interfere,' explains Tiwary.

'Where does the news come in from?' we ask Dr Tiwary. He informs us that they subscribe to a few news agencies, including ANI (Asian News International) for Supreme Court and legal news and AP (Associated Press) and Reuters for international news. The rest of the news items come from their own correspondents. Additionally, he adds that they also pick up items from the BBC while others trickle in from the monitoring of bulletins from other countries. However, this is not a usual or routine source of information.

AIR has almost fifty full-time correspondents, a mix of permanent and contractual employees posted in various cities and regional units. It also has well over a thousand part-time correspondents paid on the basis of items accepted from them. They are primarily in the districts and file their articles with the regional head, who edits them and makes them a part of the regional bulletin or sends them to the central pool, if appropriate.

We meet Sunil Gatade, a veteran journalist and a retired deputy general manager of the Press Trust of India. He is a man who speaks very softly and always waits to absorb whatever is said, before responding. He agrees with us about the reliability of AIR news.

'Post-retirement, I never miss the morning news on my radio,' says he. 'I know what I hear will be most reliable and verified.' He tells us that the weakness of the news-gathering process at AIR is that it does not have enough feet on the ground. He says that PTI has about seventy correspondents in Delhi, whereas AIR has hardly a dozen and he wonders how they manage.

Dr Tiwary counters this by stating that this comparison is invalid since PTI also has to write opinion pieces and articles where AIR broadcasts only headlines. He adds that all major news agencies have correspondents only in the main cities where NSD has part-timers up to the district and taluka level, giving them hyperlocal reach.

There was no way we could have met an official of PTI and not asked him about the controversy surrounding the termination of its contract by Prasar Bharati, so we ask Gatade about it and he first updates us on the background.

The Press Trust of India is India's largest news agency, owned by ninety-nine media organizations holding approximately 5,500 shares. It was the most significant source of news items for the NSD from the early '50s until Prasar Bharati terminated the contract in 2020, which many claim was on flimsy grounds. The termination was oft-quoted as a prime example of 'right-wing bias' and 'arbitrary action'.

Gatade loses his calm when asked about this and becomes agitated. He waves his arms about, as he tells us that Prasar Bharati wanted to dictate editorial policy. 'They wanted us to crawl on editorial matters,' he says. 'Whereas we did agree to bend, it was not enough for them, so they threw us out!'

We ask Dr Tiwary to clarify and he mentions the infamous 'Galwan interview' with the ambassador to China conducted by a

PTI correspondent. Some parts of the interview showed India in a poor light and completely countered the Indian government's stand that the aggressor in the border skirmishes at Galwan was China. The Chinese embassy put these on their social media handles, which worked against India's interests. Though PTI did clarify the matter later, stating that the Chinese embassy took the answers out of context, the episode did dent the interviewer's credibility and by association, PTI's.

'It was an anti-national act and there was no way we, being the public service broadcasters to the nation, could deal with an agency perpetrating such an act.' Tiwary leans forward as he says this and his countenance leaves no doubt about how strongly he feels on the matter. However, he adds that this was not the only case and that a few PTI correspondents had also put up many pro-Pakistani pieces and the current event was just the last straw.

We think both versions are too simplistic and linear and ask around but do not get any but the most biased responses based on known political positions. So, either the act is anti-national and deserving of the suspension or it was an arbitrary act against an organization with impeccable lineage—there is nothing in between!

We turn to YouTube and find an interview with M.K. Razdan, ex-CEO of PTI, wherein he says that PTI had 'told him' that they did not even ask the questions the Chinese put up on their website. However, he also says that he 'had heard' that PTI had asked a lot of probing follow-up questions too, which he says they, for some reason, 'did not include' in the interview they put out. How probing follow-up questions were asked for questions that were not asked at all mystifies us. He is, however, right in stating that tarring the entire organization as anti-national was not appropriate.

An article in *The Indian Express* taken from the net tells us that Samir Kumar, head of Prasar Bharati News Service, whom we had met before, had signed the letter about national interest being compromised. A reference in the very same article also states the annual billing by PTI on Prasar Bharati was ₹9.1 crore, of which 25 per cent had been held back every year since 2017 pending negotiations.

This information makes us wonder if there was a commercial dispute behind the termination and we decide to confront Samir with this and dig deeper.

'Intense negotiations were on between Prasar Bharati and PTI since April 2019,' Samir informs us. 'PTI asked us for a higher price, whereas we asked them to justify their current pricing and explain why we were being charged more for the same services than others.'

As per its pricing policy, PTI charges its subscribers based on the recipient's reach. This meant it could charge two recipients different prices for the same inputs sent across based on the recipient's reach calculation made by them.

'We hotly contested this and asked for the same prices as were being charged to others for the same inputs besides asking them to stop charging for PTI pictures and a few other services that were never or, at best, sporadically delivered,' clarifies Samir.

Samir tells us that PTI never returned with the reasons for the differential pricing. He says, 'When we finally issued the letter of termination, it made no attempts to discuss it but merely asked when the services should be discontinued.' He also states that no explanations, as promised in *The Indian Express* interview, were ever offered by PTI for the interview with the Chinese ambassador.

Shrikant Verma, a deputy director general-level officer involved in the negotiations, confirms this.

'There was a certain arrogance in PTI's attitude, almost a sense of entitlement. It was as if they were saying that they were PTI and how dare we ask them to justify anything. This did not match our current attitude, which was more business-like and we felt we had the right to ask the questions we did,' says Verma. He also points out that the tweet of the Prasar Bharati CEO, Shashi Shekhar Vempati, after the board meeting of 15 October 2020, clearly states that the cancellation was to 'rationalize expenses on news agencies' and not for any other reason.

'If we terminated the agreement with PTI because of the Chinese ambassador's interview, why did we club UNI with it?' asks Verma. 'We terminated both agreements because they were word-by-word copies of each other and loaded against Prasar Bharati. Besides, fresh tenders are underway, and all news agencies will be invited to participate. So why is PTI scared of that?' As an aside, he tells us that PTI regularly follows up with Prasar Bharati to determine when the next tender is being issued.

We look at the effect of this decision on AIR news. First, we ask our AIR friends if the reporting quality had suffered and they respond with a firm negative.

'One of the major sources of news items is the Press Information Bureau, where all journalists congregate,' says Deepa. 'That news feed comes directly to us, as do releases by the ministries, which our correspondents follow up as required. Besides, we and all others take many news items from social media, which newsmakers use for making public pronouncements. These cover most of the requirements and the agencies we subscribe to cover the rest.'

'I agree,' says Milind. 'The quality of the news bulletins has stayed the same.'

In case, as stated, there has been a tremendous cost saving without affecting the quality of the bulletin, then the bases seem covered.

We ask Milind next about the disappearance of the regional news units. His response is, 'Right from the inception of the News Services Division, the national bulletins in all the languages were continuously broadcast from Delhi and stations in the states covered regional news. So there was better coordination and a single general newsroom could cater to all of them. But despite the advantages, in 2017–18, most of the language units were transferred to the respective regional headquarters. This action upset the status quo for many and there were protests galore; delegations met the minister, sit-ins were staged, parliamentarians asked questions in both Houses and conspiracy theories were bandied about, Neelesh ji.'

Deepak Dholakia held a press conference in which he alleged that the entire exercise was carried out to help Hindusthan Samachar, the 'right-wing backed' news agency. The allegation was that the agency had proposed opening bureaus in all state capitals to provide news to the regional units and reap its benefits. However, this does not pass the litmus test because Hindusthan Samachar was and continues to be a minor player, providing news only in a few local languages. The explanation offered by Deepak is that Hindusthan Samachar was unable to cope or subsequently found it to be economically unviable and backed out, leaving AIR with an embarrassing situation it could not reverse.

The in-charge of regional bulletins, Arush Bansal, additional director-general, gives us the official view. 'We were short of talent in Delhi and were not getting new voices. Also, the newsreaders working in the units had lost touch with the nuances of their languages and often mispronounced words. So, we took this step to shore up quality,' he tells us.

Usha Joshi, retired head of the Marathi news unit, contests this version. 'We never got any complaints about our diction and pronunciation. If there was no talent, why were there so many applicants every time a panel of casual artistes was formed?' she asks.

G. Hanunath, a serving newsreader-cum-translator from Bengaluru, tells us that the quality of the national bulletins in the regional languages has suffered because of the transfer of the units to state capitals, since coordination has suffered.

'Clarifications are also difficult to seek and errors creep in. The coordination between units to learn the pronunciation of different words in different languages is no longer possible. Sometimes, due to differing priorities, the national news items are followed by district-level news in the same bulletin, which does not seem smooth,' Hanunath concludes.

There were protests from the staff of the existing regional units, who were now burdened with the extra work of handling the national bulletins with just a marginal increase in staff strength. The discontent also affected the quality of the broadcast.

The transfer of language units seems to have been an exercise in which something was lost and nothing was gained. It is unclear why AIR carried it out. It looks like a decision taken by someone without deep consideration, which AIR could not reverse for reasons of organizational prestige.

What is verifiable is that the NSD, Delhi, broadcasts the national news in English, Hindi, Urdu, Sanskrit, Punjabi and Kashmiri. The reason for retaining the first four in Delhi is that these are languages spoken all over the country. The reason for Kashmiri was security concerns and for Punjabi, it was technical.

Additionally, many foreign language programmes continue to be recorded in Delhi and relayed from terrestrial transmitters digitally through the app and uploaded to YouTube. The insiders call these the ESD languages, meaning the languages whose programmes were a part of the External Services Division, which merged with the News Services Division at the end of 2020. Many have given us the feedback that this was a precursor to closing it down. We explore the role of the External Services Division and why the merger elicited controversy.

The British government formed the External Services Division a little before the Second World War. The objective behind starting it was to counter the propaganda of the Axis powers and it had Italian, Japanese and German bulletins in addition to English news, giving the British worldview.

'This was in keeping with the worldwide trend of using radio as a tool for counter-propaganda,' explains retired Prof. Akanksha Sharma, who specialized in international politics and world history. 'In Palestine, both sides used their clandestine radio stations for this purpose in 1938. Similarly, from 1948 to 1950, several pro-communist and anti-communist groups broadcast over the air in Slovakia, Yugoslavia, Italy, Greece, Turkey and Spain. Basque separatists also set up radio broadcasting during this period, as did anti-fascists in Portugal. Radio use in revolutionary and independence movements stimulated the creation of even more stations, including stations broadcasting for liberation set up in Iraq, Iran, Lebanon, Algeria, Jordan, Syria and the Congo. From 1965 to 1967, radio broadcasting continued to spread to war zones in Asia, including Laos, Vietnam, Thailand, and Indonesia,' she elaborates.

'Initially a part of the News Services Division, ESD was spun off as a separate entity in 1948 and became a powerful tool for propagating the Indian national interest and broadcasting a mix of entertainment and news over the years. It was heard all over the world and particularly in the neighbouring regions. The Urdu service was particularly interesting and was heard extensively in Pakistan,' Sharma explains.

Obaid Niazi, who also handled the Urdu service for some time, recalls what Ghulam Ali, the noted Pakistani ghazal singer, had once told him. He said he would make his disciples listen to the AIR Urdu service to understand how to speak Urdu correctly—such was its credibility and popularity. At its peak, in the '80s, it received almost four lakh letters of appreciation every year, of which nearly 50,000 were from Pakistan.

ESD's moment of glory was during the war for the liberation of Bangladesh when it set up a makeshift studio in a rented house in the heart of Kolkata. From here, Bangladeshi poets, authors and activists broadcast to the people of Bangladesh under the banner of the Swadhin Bangla Betar or Free Bangla radio. The broadcasts bolstered the morale of a beleaguered population facing genocide and brought them up to date on the latest news. Those involved insist they were broadcasting hope. Covertly, the Indian government used it to convey, in code, information on the troop movements of the Pakistanis to the Mukti Vahini guerrillas fighting behind enemy lines, which acted as a force multiplier for them.

'Both the provisional Bangladeshi government and our authorities felt that they needed a radio station to carry on psychological warfare over the airwaves and keep up the morale of the comrades in Bangladesh. This Kolkata station resulted from that belief,' said retired IPS officer and security consultant Shantanu Mukherjee.

Given the illustrious pedigree of the ESD, we wonder why attempts were being made to close it down. However, when asked about it, Shashi Shekhar Vempati, CEO of Prasar Bharati for five years till 2022, denied this.

'The entertainment programmes can now be easily accessed through the NewsOnAir app and we have the statistics to prove that Vividh Bharati is heard all across the globe. What was left were the news and current affairs programmes. These were functioning without editorial control and the head of the ESD could arbitrarily decide to broadcast anything. It was also a zero-revenue service, so we merged it with NSD,' he says. Vempati passes it off as a part of the rationalization process necessary for creating a slim and trim organization.

We ask Shrikant Verma, the retired deputy director-general we had spoken with about PTI, to ascertain the truth. He is candid enough to admit that though ESD had an illustrious lineage, it had become moribund over time. 'There was also a lot of nepotism in it,' he admits. 'There was a well-entrenched system of patronage and certain empanelled "experts" often expressed views totally at variance with the opinions expressed by the News Services Division, causing the broadcaster to hold two viewpoints. There was also the infamous case of the ESD head who repeatedly featured in programmes, a book his father had written. Such things needed to be put down and stopped entirely with this changeover.'

We ask Dr Tiwary whether any ESD channels had been closed down and he replies with a strong negative.

'Far from closing down anything, we have increased the transmission time for each language. Whereas all the languages previously used only one channel of transmission, i.e., the terrestrial transmitters, we currently have a separate channel on YouTube for each language. In addition, the transmissions are accessible through the app, the DRM channel and FreeDish. As a result, access has increased and all the complaints we used to get regarding the transmission not being properly heard have gone down. The criticism that we have tuned down Urdu broadcasts is absolutely unfounded. We have not only increased the time for Urdu but also started a new shortwave station near Amritsar to beam our signals into Pakistan.'

We check out News Services Division website to find the links for all the language services. The World Service YouTube channel has 2.28k subscribers as of January 2022 and adding those to the terrestrial and digital listeners adds up to a sizeable number. We note that the entire gamut of the 'ESD languages', viz., Dari, Baluchi, Nepali, Mandarin, Arabic, Indonesian, Burmese, Sindhi, French, Swahili and Tibetan are represented. The Urdu service is also there in all its glory and we savour some lovely soulful ghazals as we click on the various other links.

Dr Tiwary tells us that each language now has three hours of programming and that broadcast time has doubled for all the languages spoken in the immediate neighbourhood of India. The news bulletins are now specially curated for the target areas and many programmes of local interest have been introduced. These include a news-based programme in Nepali, *Afghanistan ki Baat*, and a China and Tibet review. Besides this, the Dalai Lama's teachings and a programme on Bodhisattva's way of life are regularly beamed to Tibetan listeners. Tiwary cites a recent interview with the Nepali ambassador and an interview with the Afghan ambassador in Pushto, English and Hindi as something that only AIR could have done. He also briefs us about the plans for introducing Sinhalese and Myanmarese news and infotainment programmes in the days to come.

'Now we have a consistent narrative in all the programmes and the official public broadcaster of India is not seen as working at cross purposes. Of course, there is a bit of noise about the merger since it is, after all, a change, and any alteration of the status quo hits some interests, but time will show that it was for the better,' Tiwary concludes.

The only hassle seems to be that the transmission hardware needs upgradation, which is not happening. However, despite this glitch, the ESD merger appears to be a 'work in progress'. Hence, wait and watch is the best tag we can assign to it.

The image of the news being read from storyboards in which editors scribble changes manually sticks to our minds. We wonder if technology offers any solutions and quiz Samir Kumar again. As part of its responsibilities as a digital platform, his organization is working on developing and upgrading various software for use by Doordarshan and AIR.

He tells us that the future newsroom will see a total break from its existing form with an increasing infusion of the latest technologies. He informs us that the software currently installed in the GNR for developing bulletins online has become defunct because of external support issues. His unit had developed an indigenous software called the News Room Computer System or NRCS.

'This was in the trial stages and aimed at enabling bulletin creation and editing online and giving access to it to new units across the country, giving homogeneity to all bulletins. We wanted to conduct trials in the PBNS newsroom and after successfully trying it, push for its acceptance in the GNR of both AIR and Doordarshan. We had sought sanction to purchase computers for running this in the PBNS newsroom when the empire struck back and closed us down.' He shrugs as he says this, leaving no doubt about his disappointment.

He also tells us of the New Data Management System, or NDMS, developed internally by his unit. This system allowed all the correspondents, regional teams and stringers to upload the items on to a central database and simultaneously access it.

'Formerly, a news item filed by a stringer in a district of Maharashtra was either available to the Pune regional unit or the GNR if forwarded by the RNU. It was certainly not available to say, Kolkata,' explains Samir. 'The NDMS enabled all regional news units to access all news items and decide which ones they required. Thus, every news item has a vaster audience and access is more straightforward and real-time.'

He tells us that the content was already available with the News Service Division and Doordarshan News, but the access was now universal.

'Many news units of AIR had started taking items from the NDMS for preparing bulletins, particularly those from relatively inaccessible locations,' says Samir.

'We can even store specific news bytes that now include videos and sound bites and use them for other programmes later. We expected all the news to be uploaded and picked up from NDMS and bulletins prepared on NRCS in a few years.' He stops and the shrug says it all once again.

It is apparent that there are many glitches in the acceptance and use of technology and many turf battles and ego hassles probably need sorting out before the systems begin to play in sync.

Nowhere is this more apparent than that Prasar Bharati News Service and News Services Division of AIR, both units of Prasar Bharati Corporation, had separate websites and Twitter handles carrying the same content. Even the names of the websites were similar. Whereas PBNS was at www.newsonair.com, NSD was at www.newsonair.gov.in. Similarly, Twitter handles @PBNS-India for PBNS and @airnewsalerts for NSD carry identical tweets. Post the de facto closure of PBNS, the PBNS website now redirects to the NSD website and the PBNS Twitter handle has been inactive since August 2023. That is turf war for you!

The advent of newer technologies may signal a new way of generating bulletins. Still, the emphasis would always have to continue to be on the sincerity and dedication of its newsreaders. We mentioned to Milind the unfortunate incident of a Doordarshan news anchor getting fired as she mispronounced the Chinese premier Xi Jinping as 'eleven' Jinping!

'She wasn't coached by greats like Melville, Barun Haldar and others!' he quips. We couldn't but agree more as we turn to talk to other greats about another popular genre of broadcasting—the commentary.

3

The Spoken Word: Sports Commentary

'MY NAME HAD BEEN ANNOUNCED. THEN, WITH JUST FOUR seconds to go before going live, I saw the engineer in the control room tear away the tape of the programme from the player, which had apparently malfunctioned, throw it on the ground and collapse in his chair! Before I could react, I was live on national radio with lakhs waiting to hear the "sports round up", a thirty-minute programme on AIR. I had the unenviable task of filling in the time extempore—no script, no notes—just me and the mic. The producer across the glass panel stared at me, his face aghast, not knowing how it would shape up. But I began, purely from my recollection of what the tape had in it, went on for thirty minutes and completed it without a single fumble,' chuckles Ghaus Mohammad, the famous football commentator, as he recalls that day. 'I was not Ghaus Mohammad then: I was AIR! I couldn't afford to let AIR lose its prestige. So I just had to make it work,' he adds modestly.

This association with the medium and the adoration of it, is something one often hears while talking to sportscasters, whether they be veterans like Novy Kapadia, Sushil Doshi,

Ravi Chaturvedi, Dr Narottam Puri, B.P. Ojha, Anupam Gulati and Ghaus Mohammad, or the younger breed like Sachin Chatte and Prasanna Sant.

'Radio made cricket a religion in India,' says Novy Kapadia, and everyone seems to agree. The game introduced to us by the English was once played by royals like Ranji Jam Saheb of Nawanagar, Vizzy-Maharajkumar of Vizianagaram, the two Nawabs of Pataudi and Maharaja of Dungarpur, amongst others. It became a household name only due to AIR.

Everyone we spoke to for this book, whether commentators or fans, mentioned the golden era in the '70s when transistors shrunk in size, people could carry them around and people walking on the road with hands holding transistors glued to their ears became a common sight. Many fondly recalled how they smuggled tiny transistor sets into classrooms and offices.

There was a time when one could walk through markets and hear commentary playing in every shop. Pulokesh Mukhopadhyay, a veteran sports journalist and sports editor of *The Statesman*, remembers the streets of Kolkata he walked as a young man where the commentary blared forth from every handcart on the road, with cheers going up in unison in the entire market when a run or a goal was scored. 'When AIR covered the IFA shield matches, the entire city of Kolkata would come to a standstill, as fans sat glued to their transistor sets listening to the commentary,' he says.

Veteran Hindi commentator, Sushil Doshi, recollects a tea stall owner in Chandni Chowk in Old Delhi telling him that sales always went up three times when matches were on, as people stopped to listen while sipping hot tea. '*Kya score hua*? (What is the score?)' was the most common question one heard on the streets. Listening to sports on the radio has not reduced in popularity. With the internet available on every smartphone, scores are accessible at one's fingertips, yet the charm of listening to radio commentary remains.

The world over, sports broadcasts, or sportscasts as they are called, consist on the one hand of periodic summaries of results of sports events and comments on them by sportscasters and players, referred to as the 'sports round-ups' and on the other of live reporting of sports events—the commentary.

While 'sports round-up' has its listener base, the live commentary links the fans intimately with the game of their choice and is at the centre stage of sports coverage on radio.

We chat with Vijay Lokapally, a sports journalist for many decades and an author.

'The first radio commentary was aired in 1922 in Australia,' he tells us. 'The match covered was a testimonial for the English-born Australian test cricket player, Charles Bannerman. BBC introduced commentary in 1927, covering an England vs Wales rugby match and a cricket match played by Essex against the visiting New Zealand team. The latter would qualify as the first international match covered by radio.'

He gives us some interesting insights, 'In the pre-Second World War days, for matches played in England, the correspondent covering the games sent a ball-by-ball report by telex to a studio in Sydney, where the commentators brought it to life based on the description received. They struck a pencil on a table to give the feel of the bat meeting the ball and an assistant added the crowd's roars as sound effects. This was referred to as synthetic cricket and was quite popular. Starting in 1934, this lasted till 24 June 1938, when BBC broadcast a live ball-by-ball commentary of the second Test match of the Ashes series between England and Australia.'

In India, radio commentary was first aired in 1934 from Mumbai, covering a quadrangular tournament between Muslim and Parsi teams. The commentator was Bobby Talyarkhan, who, along with Pearson Surita, Devraj Puri, Anant Setalvad, Berry Sarvadhikari, Ashish Ray, Surajit Sen and Vizzy, dominated the field for many years. Together, they set impossibly high standards in bringing alive happenings in the stadia, with their exemplary use of language and impeccable diction.

Internationally, the game was enriched by commentary by John Arnold, called 'the poet' for his lyrical style, the Australian Alan McGilvray, who covered every test played by Australia from the mid-'40s to the mid-'80s, and John Arlott, an Englishman, who covered matches for England from the '40s to the early '80s. Classic comments like 'the stroke of a man knocking a thistle top off with a walking stick,' as Arlott described a stroke by Clive Lloyd, are recalled by cricket fans even today. Humour and sarcasm, always a part of live commentary, found their expression in comments like the one made by Richie Benaud for Glenn McGrath when the latter got out for two runs. Benaud called it getting out 'just 98 runs short of his century'. Eventually, commentators began to earn cult status and radio commentary was followed by millions worldwide.

In this period, both telling rambling stories during commentary and describing the match ball-by-ball in great detail were the orders of the day.

The acknowledged master of the 'rambling stories' style was 'Vizzy', the Maharajkumar or Prince of the princely state of Vizianagaram, now a district of Andhra Pradesh. He captained the India cricket team touring England in 1936. However, the tour was full of controversies, mainly centred on his clashes with senior players and ended in India being mercilessly thrashed by England. Surprisingly, he was knighted at the end of it. He returned the knighthood when India attained Independence and went on to an alternate career as a politician and a cricket commentator.

Dr Narottam Puri, a surgeon with a passion for sports, who has become one of the best-known faces and voices of sports coverage, chuckles as he describes the way Vizzy did commentary. 'I spent a long time with him in the commentators' box. He used to have a personal scorer and the one provided by AIR. Vizzy would describe the first ball of the over and then divert to describe past events and other stories, coming back to the game only when a coin was pressed into his palm by his scorer. The scorer was employed to hand over a coin to Vizzy under the table to remind him to return to the present! Suddenly, the listener would hear Vizzy say, "Meanwhile, two wickets have fallen and 15 runs have been scored."

A counterpoint lay in Bobby Talyarkhan, who insisted on delivering the commentary the whole day alone. He would describe the field, the run-up, the expression on the bowler's face and the thud of the bat thwacking the ball in so much detail that it would come alive in the listeners' minds.

Puri fondly recalls names like Balu Alaganan, Dicky Rutnagur and Anand Rao as great commentators. He particularly commends Dicky Rutnagur, a sports journalist, for having had extensive knowledge of the game of cricket, and says he had a good repertoire.

But the commentary in English was understood and followed only by a handful. It had not yet reached villages and the streets and lanes of each town, nor acquired cult status.

Hindi would be needed to make this happen.

In 1960, the Government of India decided that all important sports events would also be covered by Hindi commentary. Due to a plethora of greats dominating the live commentary in English, many wanting to enter the field were ignored.

One such was twenty-three-year-old Ravi Chaturvedi, a zoology lecturer at Delhi University, who couldn't get a chance as an English commentator. So he grabbed the opportunity and did the first Hindi commentary for a Ranji trophy semi-final between Delhi and Mumbai.

'I still remember the date—24 February 1961; Mumbai won by an inning and 203 runs,' he tells us. 'This was, however, broadcast only locally. It was the first Test match with Hindi commentary when India, led by the Nawab of Pataudi Jr., drew against the English team led by Ted Dexter, which brought a change in Indian sports across the country.'

The match played on 1 December 1961 in Kanpur, however, brought about a revolution. With a single masterstroke, the Hindi commentary, cricket entered millions of Indian homes in villages and cities. The sport was never the same again. India had discovered a new religion.

Chaturvedi went on to play the lion's share in popularizing Hindi commentary and cricket in India and has, to date, written twenty-seven books on cricket and cricket commentary. He is the only commentator to have completed a doctoral thesis on cricket and was also awarded a Padma Shri, the fourth highest civilian award by the Indian government in 2012. He is also a freelance journalist and writes regularly on environmental and developmental issues. The residents of his ancestral village, Dalipnagar, near Kanpur, recollect his stellar contribution to getting electricity to the village, a road connected to the highway and the de-silting of canals to provide irrigation water to the farmers.

Chaturvedi recalls how Shiv Sagar Mishra, the son-in-law of Hindi poet Ramdhari Singh Dinkar, asked him to speak pure Hindi.

'You have to find words for all field positions,' Mishra, then a station director in AIR, had insisted. Joga Rao, who later became a sportscaster, challenged Mishra to tell him the Hindi equivalent of the field position 'slip'. It soon dawned on them that the word 'parchi' or a slip of paper would sound ridiculous and they didn't know how to proceed. Finally, Chaturvedi stepped in and gave his views as a zoology lecturer. 'In science conferences worldwide, it is common to stick to the original Latin, German or English words, as the case may be. We cannot translate square leg and short leg positions to "chaukon taang" and "choti taang", can we?'

The argument settled the matter, and a truce was declared, accepting the original names of field positions.

A few years later, in 1968, another voice that significantly impacted the airwaves and created a unique position in the listeners' minds entered the field purely by default. It was the voice of Sushil Doshi, a boy from a middle-class family, who remembers watching his first cricket test match when he was a boy of fourteen. His father took him to the stadium in Mumbai but, unable to get tickets as the same were sold out, hung around the entry gate for two full days before a policeman on duty took pity on him permitted him to enter. Then, finally, he entered the stadium and his world was never the same again! An engineer by profession, Doshi, still sprightly at seventy-seven, recalls walking into the AIR office in Mumbai at twenty-five and asking to be allowed to do the commentary.

'The station director just looked at me and asked me to return when I had more grey hair,' he recalls. But as destiny would have it, faced with a deadline and no one else available, the station director had to eat crow and somehow traced Doshi to Indore and offered him the assignment.

Doshi deliberately left the cricketing terms as they were in English, but having played cricket himself, he decided to use the knowledge of the game to his advantage.

'I knew what a batsman does before he hits a shot for the boundary. So, for a square cut, I knew that the batsman removes himself from the line of the ball, makes space for the stroke and then cuts it to the boundary.' So, I went on to explain this in my commentary. It would go something like this: *Short pitch gend thi, off stump ke bahar back foot par gaye, stroke ke liye jagah banayi aur bahut khubsoorti ke saath square-cut kardiya ... char run-o ke liye.*'

Doshi went on to win the Padma Shri in 2016 and is the only commentator in India to have a commentator's box named after him. He proudly tells us that the one in the Holkar International Stadium in Indore is called the Sushil Doshi box. He has written two books, one a work of fiction based on cricket called *Cricket ka Mahabharat* and the other an autobiographical narration of his experiences as a commentator.

No mention of the golden age of commentary can be complete without mentioning the all-time great Jasdev Singh. His contribution to popularizing sportscasts is unparalleled; he did for hockey what others did for cricket—he brought it to millions of homes.

His commentary, '*Aur lambi seeti baj gayee ... aur iske saath hi Bharat ne teesra Vishwa Cup hockey ka khitaab jeet liya!* (The final whistle has blown and India has won the third Hockey World Cup!)', was heard by millions in India who rejoiced on hearing that India had won the finals against Pakistan 2-1 in the third Hockey World Cup in Malaysia in 1975. At a ceremony at Prime Minister Indira Gandhi's residence, the PM complimented Jasdev for the coverage. She searched him out and said, '*Aapne to ek baar hamari sansein hi rok dee thi, lekin jab aapne commentary mein bataya ki Bharat jeet gaya hai to maano saans phir se chalne lagi.* (You made us hold our breaths for one moment! When we heard your voice saying India had won, we could breathe again.)'

Jasdev Singh, who also did commentary for the Republic Day parades for forty-eight straight years, got the Padma Shri in 1985 and the Padma Bhushan in 2008. However, his crowning glory was winning the Olympic Order, the highest award bestowed by the International Olympic Committee. Jasdev retired as the deputy director-general at AIR, overseeing the Sports Division. His most significant contribution to sportscasting came in 1982 when India hosted the Asian Games, but more of that later.

Hindi commentary was now in overdrive and entered every Indian home, whether a tiny city apartment or a village hovel.

Doshi proudly narrates the story of walking out of a Nariman Point housing complex and being surprised to see children playing cricket, mimicking his commentary style. This was, after all, an area in which kids hardly spoke Hindi. Yet, his commentary had made an impact.

So complete was the bonding of radio with sports that commentators would often become quasi-team members.

'It was amazing how well [Jasdev Singh] identified us in a crowd on the hockey field. We considered him part of our team because he was always travelling with us,' remembers Ajitpal Singh, captain of the team that won the 1975 World Cup in Kuala Lumpur.

When teams went abroad, commentators and players would get fans' letters. In one tour of Australia, Doshi says he received 300 letters on match days, more than most players got. An apocryphal story talks of an instance when Jasdev Singh helped a visually challenged man cross the street in Lahore who recognized him because of his voice!

So spectacular was the response to Hindi that commentary was soon introduced in regional languages like Bangla, Marathi, Tamil and Telugu. Pakistan followed suit and introduced it in Urdu, Sri Lanka in Sinhalese and South Africa began broadcasting in the local language, Xhosa.

Though AIR only covered cricket and hockey in sports broadcasting initially, it also embraced other sports. Football had its fan base, as had volleyball. Until the '60s only semi-finals and finals of major tournaments, primarily football and hockey, were covered, but in the early '70s, even quarter-finals began to be covered. Davis Cup matches in which India featured were also put on the roster from the '70s.

'Why only these sports?' we asked around. The explanation came from Novy Kapadia, who believed some sports are more radio-genic than others.

Novy Kapadia started doing commentary in 1980 purely out of his love for football and covered many sports, including hockey, table tennis and athletics. Over the years, he covered and wrote about major football tournaments from all over the world. He had all the statistics about football at his fingertips and also wrote books like *Barefoot to Boots* and *The Football Fanatic's Essential Guide*, amongst others. Unfortunately, he was extremely unwell when we contacted him. Yet, he was prompt to respond and made his medical attendant hold the receiver of his landline to his ears as he spoke to us, often breaking for an hour after ten minutes of talking. One of our biggest regrets is that we did not meet him in person, as he passed away during the pandemic. 'It is tough doing commentary for table tennis, for instance,' he had explained. 'The game is so fast that one cannot do a ball-by-ball commentary. Instead, you can only speak of the game and how it is going, describe the serving style, speed, distance from the table, etc., and then give the score. I have found doing commentary for table tennis most exhausting since the concentration level required is too much to handle unless you are physically very fit.'

He went on to add that some sports are likewise too slow, citing billiards as an example. 'Even in tennis, a radio commentator continuously speaking is objected to by players,' he stated, giving the example of when Leander Paes paused his game to ask the radio commentator to stop speaking.

He informed us that even now, all major tournaments for football and hockey are covered, though only the finals are broadcast live. In addition, AIR also covers kabaddi, badminton, tennis, table tennis and all the Olympic sports at national and international levels.

Commentary in local languages at the regional level also thrives and this decision-making is decentralized. For example, commentary from Delhi on national and international sports events where the Indian team is playing is coordinated. In contrast, the local stations take a call on which matches would interest their listeners and allot time to them accordingly for regional tournaments. Examples could be a boat race in Kerala, a football match in Kolkata or a wrestling tournament in Maharashtra. Each of these is of local interest and the respective stations decide their coverage.

Allocation is also based on the availability of local airwaves. If a single channel is available, the stations have to look at previous commitments of other programmes and weigh them against the revenue and listenership options of the commentary before deciding the priority.

While the live commentary is the backbone of sportscasts on AIR, regular national and local sports are also covered in the regional sports round-ups. Lasting ten to fifteen minutes, they go by names like *Khel Sewa*, *Khel Jagat* and similar expressions in the local languages. They cover sports events of interest only locally. A national-level sports magazine is also broadcast in English and Hindi twice a month. However, live commentary takes centre stage and the commentators remain celebrities today.

'Who gets to occupy the coveted commentator spot on AIR and how is this organized?' we ask.

'Aspiring commentators send twenty-minute audio clips to AIR and are shortlisted based on it and empanelled if found suitable in subsequent interviews,' explains Dharmendra Chaurasiya, programme executive (sports) with AIR.

'Besides the knowledge of the game, which is a must, command over the language, presence of mind and confidence in one's abilities are core requisites for being empanelled,' he elaborates.

AIR has a panel of around 100 commentators organized, based on their expertise in particular sports, placed in regional, national and international panels and promoted based on ability and experience.

Whereas most commentators stick to the sport they know best, some exceptional ones are knowledgeable about more than one sport and occasionally do panel hop. Sachin Chatte and Prasanna Sant, amongst the younger set, cover multiple sports. Everyone is supposed to multitask during important events like the Asian Games and Olympics. Assignments are given purely on a rotational basis and there is hardly any radio commentator worth his salt today who has not taken this pathway on the road to stardom.

Whereas this system found approval from almost everyone, Dr Puri struck a note of dissent. 'This system of allotting matches based on rotation results in the "good" and the "not-so-good" getting lumped together.' He says the senior commentators don't get to develop their constituency.

On being asked how their skill sets evolved while on the radio, commentators had nothing but praise for describing the value added to their skills by the medium. Whereas Dr Puri says he learnt the importance of time, Chatte and Sant admit their confidence and presence of mind enhanced after being commentators.

'Purity of language, diction, the pauses, laying of emphasis at the right time, raising and lowering the volume to generate a buzz—everything about my speaking abilities is a gift from AIR,' says Chaturvedi, nodding his head vigorously to emphasize the point.

'Radio is a university and an institution which has made us what we are today. AIR has created a formal platform for many commentators to become experts,' concurs Doshi.

A quantum leap in sports coverage on radio took place at the Asian Games in 1982 when Jasdev Singh, in charge of sportscasting for radio, decided to cover all sports for the event held in Delhi. No one had ever attempted something of this type in India and neither skill sets nor templates were available. So, with national pride at stake, AIR pulled out all the stops and organized a massive programme wherein all commentators were sent to the National Institute of Sports, Patiala, for training. Every evening was filled with theory lessons and when the athletes practised, commentators would sit with coaches who would explain the sport's nuances. They were then asked to do mock commentary of the practice sessions, which the coaches monitored for technical errors.

'This resulted in an amazing skill upgrade for the commentators such as had never been attempted earlier,' says Ghaus Mohammad.

'A control room was set up at the venue with three coordinators managing it, in six-hour shifts. They kept track of the different matches at different venues and as and when a more interesting event took place at a particular venue, they would switch grounds. The commentary would then seamlessly move from one event to another. This ensured that the listeners did not miss any excitement,' explains Ghaus.

The same system carried through into the Commonwealth Games in Delhi in 2010, but the 1982 Asian Games set the benchmark. That era will always be remembered as the time when radio made a massive leap into covering Olympic events. It required a complete change in the speaking idiom since it involved discussing sports where the description of 'ball-by-ball' was impossible.

To learn more about this, we sit across the table from Raman Bhanot in his tastefully decorated office in Gurugram, near Delhi. We have known him only as the face of the live cricket analysis show *Fourth Umpire* on Doordarshan, but discover that this classically 'tall, dark and handsome' man in his mid-forties has also been a radio jockey. Looking at his profile on LinkedIn has shown us that he is as passionate about music as he is about sports. However, it is his avatar as a 'multisports commentator', as he describes himself, that we are probing right now.

'What do you describe in weightlifting?' asks Raman rhetorically. 'After all, a player comes, hoists a weight over his head and goes back; each participant does the same. Similarly, in the 100-meter dash, the commentary cannot last just twelve to fifteen seconds!'

'The trick here,' he explains, 'is to research the players' backgrounds, previous contests, the culture of the sport in the countries represented and add all these to sustain the listener's interest.'

'In weightlifting as a commentator, I learnt to describe the crowds, what the players wore, the rules for scoring points, etc. Similarly, we developed systems for the myriad events in Olympic sports and set standards for future generations to follow. So it was a baptism by fire and AIR emerged smelling of roses,' was the final verdict by Raman.

The advent of sportscasts on television in 1965 in India changed the game completely, mainly because of the advent of colour television, which came with the Asian Games. Although the first colour telecast of a sports event was a football match from Eden Gardens, Kolkata, it was the Asian Games which led to sports being telecast in full colour in a big way, nationally.

It was a great challenge for AIR since the stadium was now accessible to the viewer sitting on a sofa in his drawing room. How was AIR to match that experience and how did it cope?

Raman offers a unique explanation as he talks to us by breaking down the listeners into three categories—sports fans, fanatics and flirts. He believes the flirts were the ones to migrate to TV while the other two remained loyal to the radio.

'The core sports fans,' he says, 'still wanted to listen to the radio commentary, which offered in-depth reporting in contrast to the "rely on the screen" approach of television commentators.'

'The market for radio commentary will always exist,' maintains Prasanna Sant, a commentator from the younger lot whose father Chandrashekhar Sant pioneered Marathi commentary. 'To watch a match on television, you have to set aside everything and sit before the screen. On the other hand, a radio commentary can be heard while travelling, cooking or even in the office. Moreover, radio is the prime source of all information for those living in remote areas, where electric supply could be erratic. Also, radio is the only way for the visually challenged to connect to sports and all these categories add up to a massive number.'

He adds that students in hostels, people working the night shift and homemakers form a huge listener segment, who regularly offer feedback and ask questions. Sant credits FM channels and the subsequent development of the car radio culture for the continued popularity of the medium.

'The number of friend requests I get on social media after I do commentary or a sportscast on AIR goes up significantly after events. If no one was listening in, why would this happen?' asks Chatte, a Goa-based radio jockey and sports commentator.

Chatte talks of a match between India and the West Indies, in which he was one of the commentators. 'After the match was over at 3.30 a.m. India time, I formally announced that the expert commentator, Yashpal Sharma, would take a few questions, expecting none at that late hour. Surprisingly, the line was flooded with questions and we had to ask the listeners to stop after 4.15 a.m. And this was for a match of no significance to the series. Does this look like the response on a dying medium?' he asks, with emphasis.

'Even if the listeners have halved after the advent of television, the absolute numbers are still larger than the populations of most countries,' argues Sant.

For the moment, the television hurdle looks crossed, and the internet, which only delivers information without communicating the excitement, seems to be a distant third.

In 1991, when South Africa played their first international match at the Eden Gardens, since their suspension from international cricket in 1970, AIR faced a big challenge, which threatened the continuation of sports broadcasts. This was when Jagmohan Dalmiya controlled the activities of the Bengal Cricket Association, even before he took over as its president in 1992.

Until then, AIR covered all matches and charged a hefty fee from the Board of Control for Cricket in India. However, when

AIR's OB (outside broadcasting) vans rolled into the stadium to cover it for this match, Dalmiya had them summarily thrown out.

Some sources say that Biswanath Das, the then sports in-charge at AIR, known for his arrogant attitude, rubbed some journalists the wrong way. They conspired and planted the idea in Dalmiya's mind that nowhere in the world was a match televised in the city where it was being played as it cut into the ticket sales. Dalmiya saw this logic and found no agreement requiring him to permit AIR to broadcast the match commentary live. He then threw the national broadcaster's OB vans out of Eden Gardens. Dalmiya sold the rights of the Hero Cup matches in 1993–94 to Star TV, which ultimately made BCCI the richest sports body in the world. Even the Supreme Court offered no relief and ruled against the government in 1993, agreeing with the Cricket Associations that the commentary and televising rights were their property and could be sold to whom they liked.

Vijay Lokapally, a senior journalist working for *The Hindu*, tells how radio worked out of this situation.

'The up-linking facility was only with the ministry of information and broadcasting,' he explains. 'Whoever got the rights had to come to the I&B ministry, which arm-twisted them into letting AIR do audio commentary. In 2007, the Parliament passed a bill that made it mandatory for the rights holders to let matches of "national importance" (as defined by the government from time to time) be aired by Doordarshan on their free channel. Doordarshan could take the feed from the rights' owner and even retain the revenue generated through advertisements.'

However, this bill did not cover radio and BCCI removed the broadcast rights from the television rights in 2014 and offered them for sale separately. Suddenly, every match had to be negotiated with BCCI by AIR and agreements were often signed a day before the game began. This led to a complete dislocation of commentary until September 2019, when a two-year contract was signed between them, granting AIR audio rights on a mutually agreed revenue-sharing model for three years.

AIR was back in the commentary business once more!

But disruption always leads to innovation and a new way of doing commentary evolved—commentators would sit in studios, watch the match on television and convert what they saw into an audio commentary. Of course, they were not allowed into stadiums, but nothing prohibited them from watching the match on television and converting it to audio. It was a poor substitute, yet it was better than nothing.

'You get the whole picture when you sit in the stadium,' elaborates Doshi. 'There have been times when I have seen a lofted shot and the camera panning on the ball. But, tell me, how would I know whether the ball would land beyond the boundary or into the hands of the fielder positioned below? So the energy of the commentary suffers.'

'The fans screaming, the pin-drop silence of 80,000 spectators when a ball is bowled and the pent-up emotions when the same ball is thudded out of the field by the batsman are unbeatable experiences. I get goosebumps while reporting them. These translate into energy in the broadcast; without these, radio was no radio at all,' Sant says.

Ghaus Mohammad adds, 'In football, it is important to speak about what is happening and what could have happened. This is possible only when we are in the stadium. I see the ball on television and who it is passed to. I don't see the entire field. This affects my narrative.'

'Unless I can smell the grass and hear the thud of the bat against the ball, my commentary is not what it should be,' is the last word by Dr Puri. Thankfully this is possible as the commentator is on the ground, watching the match live.

But sportscasting would always be associated with the one doing the commentary.

Unlike when some commentators offered ball-by-ball commentary, others preferred to embellish it with stories. Today, most prefer an eclectic style. 'If a spinner bowls three maiden overs in a row and the batsman defends every ball, what do you describe?' asks Chatte. 'If it rains during the match and play is called off for a few minutes, the TV commentator has the luxury of speaking for a few minutes and then keeping quiet. However, the radio commentator has to keep the listener engaged. At this juncture, his knowledge and research come in handy.'

All the commentators we spoke to were united in their view that radio requires much more research than television, particularly in the current days when the listener has access to multiple sources of information.

'I researched the ground and city hosting the match, apart from my research on the players,' says Chaturvedi. 'For example, I would talk of the name of the Green Park grounds in Kanpur, derived from the British racing their hounds there. I would tell my listeners that the Ferozeshah Kotla grounds in Delhi has a long history of association with sports, as here, Ferozeshah Tughlaq played a polo-like game called chaugan. Such bits and pieces help fill the gaps and engage the audience.'

'With information available at the click of a mouse, adding value is critical for being a good commentator. For example, it is pointless to tell the listener that Lionel Messi is from Argentina when doing a commentary on a Barcelona match. Instead, it would be more interesting if the commentator spoke of his favourite shots, how he passes the ball and the strategy he will use that day,' says Chatte. 'But you can't do that unless you know the player intimately and the game well.'

Research, for the radio commentator, is king. The advent of the internet is the next challenge for radio commentary and AIR is upping its ante and not sitting quietly. In fact, it is embracing technology to its advantage. It now has multiple social media handles and YouTube channels, as well as the NewsOnAir app, which has over 230 radio stations available on the mobile, by which the potential reach of radio has gone up astronomically. Hardly anybody now carries a transistor, but everybody, without exception, has a mobile, which, in most cases, is a smartphone. This offers a massive listener base, by any measure.

All experts agree that good quality marketing is needed to capture this massive market. Unfortunately, the current marketing drives have been disappointing, with many sports events being dropped from the list of sports covered for not generating adequate ad revenue. Doshi sees this as the failure of AIR's marketing department.

'AIR has first to professionalize the marketing setup and then leverage the reach for revenue,' Doshi suggests.

For instance, the NewsOnAir mobile app, promoted just before an important sporting event, could catapult it to the number one source of information in no time.

'The content will also have to change keeping in tune with the times and the commentators will have to adapt to the shorter attention spans of the listeners,' feels Ghaus Mohammad.

'In cricket, scores must be told after every three or four balls and the scorecard read out at regular intervals. Besides, the commentary will need to be pacier so that people who come in for a few minutes stay longer,' says Dr Puri.

'Even now, we keep summarizing the match within a few sentences in football games; that's the way forward,' Ghaus Mohammad concurs.

'Adaptation is the way to survive and thrive,' Chatte opines. 'For sports like wrestling, educating the listener in the nuances of the sports is also crucial. For example, how many people know the rules of the Graeco-Roman style or the scoring system in modern wrestling and boxing? How many listeners can figure out the strategy used by the wrestlers or boxers? Add these and you are assured of a loyal listener base.'

'Irrespective of who you are, what you do, where you live and what social, educational and financial strata you come from, you always have access to the radio and listen to it. Radio is not going anywhere,' Sant concludes.

We are convinced that sports broadcasting will continue to thrive and grow. After all, no one gets across the drama on the field as well as radio does.

4

The Spoken Word: Plays, Poetry and Stories

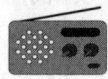

'ACTING IS MY LIFE AND SOUL, THOUGH I AM A MECHANICAL engineer by qualification. I quit a well-paying job managing an industrial unit in the early '80s to come to Mumbai to become a full-time actor. I have acted across media for over fifty years as an actor. I have done theatre, of course, but I have also acted in daily soaps and movies. However, I cannot ever repay the debt of gratitude that I owe to my time doing radio plays. I have learned everything about using my voice from the radio.'

We are speaking to S.M. Zaheer, the veteran character actor. He starred in the first daily soaps on Indian television—*Buniyaad* and *Hum Log*, and has continued to act in numerous soaps and many superhit movies like *Veer-Zaara*.

'Radio is a medium in which how I look, move or emote does not matter. It is my voice that conveys my feelings to my listeners. I have learned everything I know about voice modulation from acting in radio plays, which continues to be my strength as an actor even to date.'

We speak to many theatre actors and hear the same story. But, while those like Zaheer, who acted in radio plays in the '80s, can be described as veterans today, they were by no means the first to work on radio.

The history of plays on the radio goes back to almost the '30s, when the radio station in Lahore started broadcasting them. The themes then were existing theatre plays whose soundtracks were broadcast by AIR. In some cases, producers hung microphones on the stage, recorded exclusive performances and broadcast them verbatim. However, as theatre granted immediate recognition and better emoluments, most artistes and playwrights stayed away from the radio. Also, most of them considered broadcasting their plays as demeaning. Fortunately, most of the stage plays broadcast on the radio did not impress listeners. Gradually, the realization dawned that writing and enacting plays on the radio were separate art forms.

AIR then attempted to get plays written exclusively for radio and a contest was announced in 1936 for writing radio plays, with a prize of ₹200 announced for the best entry.

The director of the radio station in Lahore, Zulfikar Bukhari, personally lectured in colleges and conducted workshops on writing a radio script. He is once reputed to have gone for coffee and on finding a few writers assembled there, preached to them on writing radio scripts. Such was the dedication. Everyone we speak to is in total awe of Bukhari and tales of his commitment to the craft are legion. Wanting an echo of a particular sound and not being able to get it right in the studio, he once took a microphone and recorder and lowered himself into an abandoned well near the studios to record it. Whereas the going down was easy, he could not climb back and the office peon, hearing his cries, had to arrange to help pull the director sahab out!

The efforts bore fruit and gradually, authors as eminent as Harindranath Chattopadhyay, Kartar Singh Duggal, Rajinder Singh Bedi, Upendranath Ashk, Saghar Nizami, Faiz Ahmad Faiz, Raja Mehdi Ali Khan and Saadat Hasan Manto started writing plays exclusively for radio. For this, the playwrights learned to substitute dialogue for action and the actor learned to communicate emotions through vocal variations, only leading to the customizations gradually gaining effectiveness and thus popularity.

Manto wrote a play called *Aao Radio Sune*, which became so popular that he wrote a series of plays in a similar vein. Two of the most popular were *Aao Jhoot Bolein* and *Aao Chori Karein*. But, unfortunately, try as we might, we can not get our hands on these scripts.

Broadcasting plays gradually became a norm on other radio stations. In 1930, Bombay broadcast seventy-three plays in Hindustani, twenty-four in Gujarati and twenty-seven in Marathi.

Many noted artistes from the old times like Om Prakash, Balraj Sahni, Sardar Akhtar, Malika Pukhraj, Begum Akhtar, Adi Marzban, Achala Sachdev, Kamini Kaushal, Manmohan Krishna and Durga Khote, amongst others, were regulars in radio plays. Likewise, Raj Kapoor was a regular on children's programmes on the radio.

Thus, though some talented artistes migrated to or stayed in Pakistan in the post-Independence era, India had many competent playwrights and radio actors to enable the movement to be taken forward.

The year 1956 was when the broadcast of plays on the radio got a fillip with the setting up of the Central Drama Unit.

'The Central Drama Unit is one of the oldest theatre units in the country. So many actors who have passed through the studios of AIR have gone on to make a name for themselves across media,' says Amit Sharma, its current head.

Many recent stage and screen stalwarts also have, so to say, cut their teeth in radio plays. Besides Zaheer, Seema Bhargava Pahwa, Om and Sudha Shivpuri, Raj and Nadira Babbar, Habib Tanveer, Raghubir Yadav, Pankaj Kapur and Zeeshan Ayub are some of the stars of radio plays who moved from behind the microphone to the big or small screen.

We ask Amit if AIR had employed them at some point in their careers and he tells us about the empanelment system.

All actors have to take an audition. Then, based on the quality assessed by the panel and their stature and experience outside radio, they are empanelled and categorized as B, B+, A+ or Top. The producer then calls each on an assignment basis, depending on the suitability for the role in mind. When called up, they sign a limited-time contract with AIR and get paid according to their category.

'I learned to sign my name at six,' says Vandan Paranjpe, a language coach from Pune, now in her sixties. 'In the '60s, I was a regular in plays in the children's programmes on the Delhi station of AIR for almost seven years. However, my proudest moment was not when AIR aired my programmes but when I had to take out a pen and sign my contract,' she chuckles.

She is one of the thousands of currently unknown names who have learnt the art of modulating their voices from their exposure to the radio.

That there are many such names is only natural. After all, the unit has, for sixty-three years, been producing a one-hour play every month. This is part of the National Programme of Plays and is in addition to a few smaller ones made by the unit. Some plays are also produced locally or on Vividh Bharati. The original script for this is in Hindi and is recorded for the Hindi heartland. After that, the central unit sends the script to the regional stations, which translate it into the respective language and record it with local artistes. Thus, the play is simultaneously broadcast at 9.30 p.m. every fourth Thursday of the month in eighteen languages.

'The choice of plays depends on both the playwright and the theme,' Amit tells us. He is a tall, very fit man in his fifties with a salt-and-pepper beard and an energy level that someone half his age would envy.

'If a well-known author's story is being adapted, the theme is unimportant since the author's name would attract listeners. However, this method of choosing is adopted because if the author is relatively lesser-known, then the theme has to matter.'

There are, of course, times when socially relevant themes are chosen and plays are woven around them. At other times, short stories are turned into hour-long plays. We asked Amit about the themes he chooses to create radio plays.

'As a public service broadcaster, we need to have plays on socially relevant issues like saving the tiger, conserving water and such. That is our duty; hence, we often create scripts around them. But, of course, we attempt to keep them universal to fit into the social context across the country. However, sometimes, even a play with a north Indian context does well throughout the country.'

He tells us that he once aired a play called *Sindoor*. Applying sindoor or vermilion in the parting of the hair of married women is a typical north Indian custom. Hence, he had thought listeners might not appreciate this in the south. However, the underlying theme resonated with audiences across India and brought awareness of a custom from one part of the country to others.

'I have done the odd play which would raise hackles in the government too and my bosses have backed me.' Amit nods his head as he almost senses our unasked question.

He tells us that he once created a play out of interviews with freedom fighters sentenced to life imprisonment at the dreaded Andaman Cellular Jail.

'They made a lot of critical comments about the state of the nation and about how they did not sacrifice their youth for the country to get where it was. The bosses initially thought it might not go down well with the government. Still, the brass stood by me when I took a stand and said we were accountable to the public and the taxpayer and they had a right to know.' The play became a big hit and was appreciated by all.

The Central Drama Unit also produces a 'chain play' in Hindi, which is broadcast from Delhi every third Friday at 10 p.m. After the Delhi broadcast, the central unit creates the play and passes it on to the thirty-two main Hindi channel stations, which air the recordings. The sequencing is predetermined, so a play stays in circulation for six months. So when the central unit broadcasts a new play, the last in the chain broadcasts the one that was aired six months previously. The thirty-two and the relay stations attached to each ensure the play gets a larger audience than the central unit could muster alone.

We wonder if humour is a casualty in all this serious business, but a very catchy tune makes its presence felt in our minds. We are reminded of the top-rated programme *Hawa Mahal* and its instantly recognizable signature tune. The programme of fifteen-minute skits has been aired from time immemorial, at 9.15 p.m. every day on Vividh Bharati, the entertainment channel and we make a mental note to check up on it when we connect with the Vividh Bharati section in Mumbai.

Whereas plays, as we have seen, were also written primarily for AIR, classics were often adapted for radio as plays and went on to score very highly with the audiences. S.M. Zaheer, the veteran actor we have spoken to before, recalled with glee the role he played in an adaptation of *Journey to the Centre of the Earth* by Jules Verne. 'It was broadcast over several months, in episodes of ten minutes each, every Sunday, and was so engaging that the kids in the colony would ambush me when I would be getting home and ask me what would happen next,' he had told us.

Though it was primarily a story reading, descriptions of the strange sights encountered by the protagonist on the journey were transformed into dialogues to make the narration more appealing. One or two kids were a part of this, responding appropriately, making it more of a play than a story reading.

Serialized reading out of stories was an attempt made in the '50s and early '60s but did not find much prominence because the demands of the medium were such that a dramatized version always found more acceptance. Although stories would only be aired as dramatic adaptations as an unwritten rule, this thumb rule went for a toss during the recent COVID-19 pandemic.

The power of both story and AIR was brought home in the pandemic like never before. With the Coronavirus playing havoc globally, there was fear in the air and people were locked up at home. With no contact with the outside world, an atmosphere of negativity prevailed. AIR decided to take things in hand and release a wave of positivity to counter this negativity avalanche. The CEO of Prasar Bharati circulated a note amongst all units for broadcasting stories for children and suggested the name of Ruskin Bond as a possible source. The Central English Features units rose to the challenge.

'I had known Ruskin Bond during an earlier stint when I had been instrumental in helping him with regularizing some paperwork of his interactions with AIR, so I offered to contact him,' says Basudha Banerji, who was then in charge of the English Features unit.

Ruskin Bond readily agreed to read out from his book. Signing on Bond was outstanding, since his immense popularity would ensure a listenership. In addition, the nature of his stories would spread positivity.

Problems soon surfaced. How does one record a story in a total lockdown? How does one promote such an event? The innate creativity of the broadcasters and the capacity for jugaad (the ability to find innovative, frugal solutions) came to the fore to solve this problem. Bond would call on the landline every day and read a story while Basudha recorded it.

'You will be surprised to hear about my recording studio's location,' she chuckles. 'I recorded wherever I could, sometimes in the kitchen or in the bedroom with sheets hung on walls to muffle out echoes. I also enforced a strict curfew in the house to keep outside sounds away. We recorded promos in the oddest of places. Manoj recorded some in a studio created inside a mosquito net!'

We ask Manoj Atri about the recording studio and he laughs aloud, recalling it.

'My house is located right alongside a main road,' he says, 'and though the roads were not so busy then, the occasional vehicle did pass by and the sounds needed to be eliminated. So I strung up a mosquito net in my spare bedroom, covered it with bedsheets and created a recording tent.'

'Basudha and I also co-created a brand-new storytelling series, using stories from the *Panchatantra*, *Hitopadesha*, etc. The series with Bond was called *Bonding over Radio* and the second was called *Jungle Jungle Phir Baat Chali*. We took the title from the jingle in the Hindi version of Kipling's *The Jungle Book*. The original jingle was immensely popular amongst kids and drew immediate attention. So to differentiate our jingle from the original, Basudha and her team added the word "phir" to it,' says Manoj.

Manoj's daughter Sara, all of eight years, sang the signature tune, a quirky version of a tillana. The raw naughtiness came from asking a child without exposure to Carnatic music to sing it, creating an instant connection with children. The title being Hindi and the signature tune south Indian, the song projected a national ethos.

The noted lyricist Gulzar, who had penned the original, granted permission to use his lines readily, adding that they need not even have asked him, since the use was for such a good cause.

'To keep my daughter giggling through the recording to get that freshness, my wife held the microphone and I performed an old Hindi film "Helen style" dance to her singing!' Manoj reveals this and then stops mid-sentence since we are beginning to look at him, trying to imagine how he must have looked doing a 'Helen style' dance. Then, all of us burst out laughing loudly.

The fifty-four episodes of *Bonding over Radio* and the fifty-four of *Jungle Jungle Phir Baat Chali* became massive hits within the country and worldwide. As they were broadcast on the External Services frequencies and the local FM channels, listeners worldwide tuned in to listen to them. Those who missed the broadcast logged in to the YouTube channel and the Facebook page and gave enthusiastic feedback. Such was the popularity that a part of the programme inviting listeners to ask questions to Ruskin Bond had to be called off after five days since the channels got swamped with comments and questions!

A simple concept, aided by the rocket thrust of the creativity of the AIR broadcasters, had created magic yet again.

Storytelling has made a comeback on the airwaves. Neelesh Misra, broadcasting on a popular private FM channel, has achieved almost iconic status by telling heart-touching stories. His signature line, '*Mera naam Neelesh Misra hai aur main kahaniyaan sunata hoon*', has taken the world by storm and his official Facebook page has almost a million followers. However, a matching response by AIR is not visible and is awaited.

Poetry is another genre that AIR extensively covered before and is now limited to either reports in magazine sections or to occasional broadcasts by local stations.

In the post-Independence period, poets like Maithili Sharan Gupt, Suryakant Tripathi 'Nirala', Mahadevi Verma and shayars Nida Fazli, Majrooh Sultanpuri, Parveen Shakir, Irshad Kamil, amongst many notable names read out their poetry live on AIR.

Not only that, but kavi sammelans and mushairas were broadcast live on the national network. Many recall the live broadcast of the kavi sammelans and mushairas held at the Red Fort. People would sit by the radio with notebooks, noting what their favourite poets had to say. For that matter, many poets gained prominence in the '60s because listeners heard them over the radio.

It is not that the coverage has completely stopped, but it has undoubtedly been minimized and relegated to the local station level. A lack of interest in poetry could not be why people continue to throng to poetry recitations. No space for standing is available when famous poets recite their verses or are interviewed at the Jashn-e-Rekhta in Delhi. Packed auditoriums and stadiums are the venues of popular poetry events, but they no longer feature live on AIR. Maybe revenue generation is not possible from poetry recitations. Also, the cost of organizing the same has shot up astronomically as the star poets now charge appearance fees equal to those charged by film stars and hence resources are a constraint. Whatever the reason, poetry is certainly not on the primary radar anymore.

The case of the talk show is the exact opposite of poetry. Talks by eminent experts on topics in their domain were commonplace in the pre- and post-Independence days and people would flock to them as they do to concerts today. However, these faded away in the following years. The 'talk shows' on television, primarily personality-based rather than issue-based, are poor substitutes for the original talks.

AIR, however, continues to broadcast talks regularly and has a faithful niche audience.

'A talk is for the listener who wants to delve deep into any subject and includes experts speaking in detail about the topics they have mastery over,' Basudha Banerji tells us. 'A talk can consist of a fifteen-minute event that features just one person holding forth on their area of expertise or an anchor interviewing them. The latter reduces monotony, lasts thirty minutes and is more informative. A third and more exciting talk format is when a group of experts have a panel discussion on a topic.' She concludes that this needs a lot of coordination, since the experts need to be present in the studio.

Great care is taken while recording a talk for AIR. The experts are identified and asked to submit a script in advance. This is then edited or modified to suit the time slot available and then aired. Sometimes, however, when an expert is a very eminent personality, this becomes difficult and offers the greatest challenge to the producer. Asking for the script could annoy the expert and editing it more so. Yet the producer must ensure that the expert does not ramble and that the script is interesting. Since not all experts are necessarily good presenters, this task becomes more daunting.

'It is a tense moment for the producer,' says Manoj. 'We have to use diplomacy of the highest order to convince the expert that the editing will improve the effectiveness of their talk. If this does not work, we sit and bite our nails till the recording ends, making mental notes of where to snip and edit.'

'A big challenge was once faced when a professor from a university in Scotland, Prof. Chandrika Kaul, said she would talk on the history of AIR in the pre-Independence days,' Manoj tells us. 'She had not submitted a script and I was told to give her free rein. So we sat with our fingers not just crossed but locked together until she began—and then we were mesmerized. Prof. Kaul spoke for twenty-five minutes without a break, with such interesting trivia and facts thrown in that we wished it did not have to end. We played the talk without a single cut and it was one of the most heard talks in recent times!'

'Such events are rare and a lot of editing work is involved in most talks and takes and retakes are common,' confirms Basudha.

Whereas AIR broadcasts at the regional level on local topics, the most heard programmes are the *National Programme of Talks* in

English and the *Vartaon ka Akhil Bharatiya Karyakram* programme in Hindi. These are broadcast monthly on Tuesdays, picked up by almost 100-plus stations from India and aired simultaneously, giving them vast reach.

The Central Production Unit records most talks in Delhi, but there are times when experts are only available at other locations and the recordings have to take place there. In such cases, the editorial control stays in the central unit and only the recording is decentralized. So, a talk on some aspects of Tagore is best recorded in Kolkata and a discussion featuring Western music in Shillong or Guwahati. But, again, the key is the availability of experts on the topic.

'Talks are a great hit amongst students, academics and even those aspiring to join the civil services,' concludes Basudha. Amongst the plethora of talk shows on television channels, many hosted by celebrities, AIR stands out even today for its solid, well-researched content and choice of topics.

Due to its vast reach, AIR has always been used by leaders and politicians to convey essential matters to the country's people.

'Mahatma Gandhi was neither a Prime Minister nor did he hold any post. He spoke from his heart as an ordinary citizen. Therefore, his only address on AIR was the best example of public service broadcasting,' says Suhas Borkar of Jan Prasar Abhiyan, a think-tank working on public broadcasting policy. Borkar conceptualized celebrating the day Gandhi spoke as Jan Prasaran Diwas (Public Service Broadcasting Day) in 2000 and the nation continues to celebrate it even today.

Historically, radio was used extensively during war, turbulence and national emergencies. However, radio broadcasts can sometimes become a turning point in a person's life, as in the case of the celebrated author P.G. Wodehouse. The Nazis roped in Wodehouse to broadcast for them and he was immediately branded as an enemy by the British public. Though MI5 ultimately decided not to prosecute him, it seemed British citizens had already made up their minds, with some bookstores and libraries even removing all Wodehouse material from their shelves. Seeing the writing on the wall, the author and his wife packed up all their belongings and moved to New York in 1947, never to return.

Like many other leaders during the Second World War, Churchill exploited its power, though surprisingly, his 'We shall fight on the beaches, we shall fight on the landing grounds' speech was never broadcast on radio.

Within India, too, examples abide. For instance, Subhas Chandra Bose used the 'Azad Hind Radio' very effectively to rouse Indians to fight against the British.

Similarly, during the 1965 war with Pakistan, the then Prime Minister Lal Bahadur Shastri used AIR to warn Pakistan clearly. 'The Pakistanis think these dhoti-clad men cannot do anything but let me warn them that I am not as simple as I look,' he threatened.

Similarly, when he honoured the country's farmers by equating them with soldiers and gave the nation the famous slogan '*Jai Jawan Jai Kisan*', he first delivered it over AIR.

Indira Gandhi also used it to announce many important decisions, such as bank nationalization and, in 1975, the imposition of the 'internal emergency'. In her time, AIR was sarcastically referred to as 'All Indira Radio' for echoing only her point of view. However, the sycophancy went to such an extent that when she nationalized banks and declared it a pro-poor measure, AIR concentrated all its efforts on covering it and forgot to cover the lunar landing!

However, the most consistent and effective use of radio as a medium is currently being made by Prime Minister Narendra Modi. Sometime in 2014, he expressed his desire to communicate with the nation through radio. He said he did not want to talk politics in the broadcast but wanted to share some '*Halki-fulki mann ki batein*'. From this was born the series *Mann ki Baat* and he broadcast the first on 3 October 2014.

Modi spoke on a wide variety of topics, starting from the 'Swachh Bharat Abhiyan' (Clean India Campaign) launched just the day before, to the use of khadi, and quoted from Vivekananda, urging people to be aware of the tremendous potential that they had. Ganesh Venkatadri from Mumbai was the first common man featured in this series. Modi acknowledged and quoted his comments on Vijaya Dashami on the Prime Minister's office website. A suggestion from one Gautam Pal on programmes for children with special needs was also recognized. The most crucial announcement by the Prime Minister was that he would make sincere attempts to ensure that this dialogue would remain continuous. Though the first broadcast was on a Friday, Modi promised the nation that it would be subsequently only on Sundays at 11 a.m., to ensure listeners could tune in easily.

Modi spoke in Hindi, but AIR broadcast translations in ten Indian languages. The translation in English was aired later to reach non-resident Indians and foreign listeners. The seventy-eighth episode was translated and aired in twenty-seven languages, including Garo, Khasi, Jaintia, Mizo, Bodo and Santali. Unsurprisingly, the programme's reach is over fifty crore people.

Many, including AIR staffers, were surprised that Modi, considered as tech-savvy, had chosen the radio as a medium to communicate with India's 130 crore population.

'We were in a conference in Udaipur when we heard this,' says Sukhjinder Kaur, the first director of the Central Marketing Unit based in Delhi. 'All the officers from the director level upwards were present and each was presenting their ideas to the CEO, Prasar Bharati. Revenue generation was being discussed when the big news broke. The Prime Minister had chosen radio to communicate with the nation. I raised my hand to speak out, but the CEO told me to discuss whatever I wanted in Delhi since we were posted there. He asked me to let the others speak.'

She, however, continued to raise her hand till the CEO, Mr Jawhar Sircar, understood that she had something important to say and let her speak. But, not surprisingly, what she proposed shook up the audience and they all erupted with loud 'nos'.

'I proposed that we monetize *Mann ki Baat* by inserting ads in it,' she chuckles as she tells us, 'and pandemonium broke loose.'

The accusation was that she was trying to sell the Prime Minister. She, of course, refuted the argument by saying she was not proposing that AIR insert ads in between the speech but only before and after. Her view was that the reach of such ads would be phenomenal and brands requiring pan-India recognition could not ask for a better opportunity.

'As a compromise, officers present suggested that we refer the issue to the PMO, but I resisted that as it would take too much time to get approval. However, I kept at it till the CEO relented and asked me to decide on a rate card.' We started with a rate of ₹2 lakhs per ten seconds.' Though there was a proposal for premium pricing, she shot it down as that would have made the slot out of reach for most advertisers. 'Nevertheless, the programme became the biggest show ever, both in listenership and revenue generation,' she says.

'Out of the total revenue of ₹300 crore of the marketing division in 2017–18, 10 per cent came from *Mann ki Baat*,' she concludes triumphantly.

The broadcast of 27 January 2015 deviated from the Sunday broadcast norm by being beamed on a Wednesday. In this episode, Modi shared broadcast time with a friend—President Barack Obama of the United States of America. As Obama stated in it, this was the first time an American president had spoken live while sharing broadcast time with anyone. An achievement indeed!

It was also the only instance when Modi shared the time with anyone. Since then, he has spoken to students before their exams, asking them not to stress too much, to athletes after the Olympics and other sporting events, to soldiers, homemakers, children and almost every segment of society.

As the name suggests, the programme has established a connection with crores of people, as it is from the heart. Thousands of letters come into Akashvani before the programme is aired. It shows how people are getting connected not just to radio but are keen to give comments and suggestions to the country's Prime Minister. Since May 2016, *Mann ki Baat* kiosks have been set up in Pune, Varanasi, Faridabad, Lucknow, Chandigarh, Shimla, Cuttack, Bhubaneswar and others, where people can go and record their ideas and messages. Suggestions received up to two days before the broadcast are taken cognizance of and a special cell in the PMO evaluates them and puts the selected ones up to the Prime Minister for inclusion in his address.

Historian Saradindu Mukherji says, 'In our country, an overwhelming majority of people, especially in rural areas, are without a TV set and fewer still read newspapers. Narendra Modiji's reliance on the radio as the most effective means of communicating with the people constitutes using the best possible option. Modiji's choice of radio is thus a veritable symbol of his concern for the common man and a testimonial to the massive reach and potential of AIR.'

In addition to these, live sessions with experts were also the order of the day.

Historian Swapna Liddle fondly recalls her stint on FM Rainbow Channel, where she was part of a programme called *Baarish Sawalon Ki*. It was a weekly live 'call in' programme in which experts answered questions from callers on areas of their specialization. Swapna was featured twice a month initially and then once, answering questions from Delhiites on her passion, the built heritage of Delhi. People would call her to talk about monuments they had seen but could not identify or those they knew about but wanted to learn more. These were live sessions with listeners calling in real-time and being answered instantly.

'It was quite challenging,' she recalls, 'I used my familiarity with the heritage of Delhi to good advantage, but some refused to believe I was doing it live. One day, a caller asked this on air and we had to tell him he was and so were we. It was only on hearing his own voice on the radio as he spoke that he believed I was live.' She chuckles as she tells us the story. 'Most questions were about better-known monuments, but some baffled me too and I would typically promise to look up the information and answer later,' she concludes. The Features units claim that it educates people, comes across strongly and is well-established.

We have followed the spoken word enough, and it is time to turn to the other format that forms a staple of broadcasts on AIR—music. However, we must first navigate through the mixed-format programmes. These are the ones that combine music and the spoken word beautifully to engage listeners and we intend to find out more about them now.

5

The Spoken Word and the Mixed Format

'ALL MAJOR BROADCASTS ON RADIO CONSIST OF EITHER spoken words or music, don't they?' we ask Manoj Atri and Basudha Banerji, who have become friends. With their long careers with AIR, they are veterans of the broadcast world, who have moved through participating in and producing various programmes and have vast exposure to the medium.

Basudha chooses to answer. 'Yes, these are formats used for producing programmes of different kinds, either singly or in combinations. For example, a music piece can be instrumental or vocal, classical or pop, or blended to produce many variations. Similarly, the spoken word can be in the form of an anchor's narration, a discussion, a story reading, a commentary, an interview or a poetry recitation. The spoken word and music are often combined to get a mixed format like a skit or a play. Yet the play or skit consists primarily of dialogues and music is either a filler or used to enhance some emotions briefly.'

'It is in the features and the magazines that both come into their own to produce a complete audio experience,' adds Manoj.

These are two categories that are pure vintage AIR and to the best of our knowledge, no private channel has ever tried them. But AIR has been airing them with aplomb almost since inception.

'Manoj and I are work cousins,' says Basudha Banerji. 'We produce various magazines and features for AIR.'

They tell us that this work has all their creative juices flowing since they have such a vast canvas to experiment with both in terms of the themes covered and the tools used.

We are curious to understand the difference between radio magazines and features.

'The difference between magazines and features,' Basudha explains, 'is that while the magazine covers a wide variety of topics in every episode and offers an overview of many topics, the feature takes only one issue at a time and goes deep into it. As a result, the magazine stokes curiosity and the feature feeds it.'

Magazines and features use music and the spoken word to create a smooth-flowing narrative that attracts attention, educates and entertains. The variety ensures both attention to and retention of the message. For example, while reading a feature in a print magazine, you could switch off and disconnect, but with music and the narrator's voice and sound clips all intermixed, you stay engaged in a radio feature or magazine.

'You switch on and it hooks you,' exclaims Basudha with a twinkle in her eyes. It is hard to believe she is almost sixty and nearing retirement—the passion for radio lights up her face when she speaks, making her look much younger.

We mention this to her and she laughs aloud. 'I just start gushing when I speak of radio and broadcasting,' she tells us.

Basudha wanted to be a print journalist but quit that dream after moving to Delhi post-marriage, and took up a job with AIR as a transmission executive.

'The desk job as a duty officer taught me a lot but smothered my creativity. Then, one day, I walked past a room which said

"Central English Features Unit" and, on a hunch, walked in—and discovered heaven!'

She goes on about how she stood transfixed on entering the room. A giant board with numerous pictures of Melville de Mellow receiving awards and citations for producing features faced her. She goes on for a long time on how these inspired her and how she knew she had finally found her calling, but comes back with a jerk and says, 'Oh, you want to know about features, don't you? Not my story.'

She explains that a radio feature is like an article in a newspaper, which takes up an issue, highlights the related facts and considers conflicting opinions to complete the narrative.

'When I did a feature on honour killings,' she illustrates with an example, 'I trudged across Haryana and talked to the khap panchayats, the local member of Parliament, a social psychologist and a rights activist and tried to bring balance in the narrative by airing all shades of opinions.'

When Basudha's Alice delved into this wonderland, she found she could do much more with the information than a print journalist. In answer to our unasked question of how she could say this, she bids us listen to a feature on tea drinking aired by her in 2005.

We begin to listen and sit transfixed with the journey, which starts from the mythological story of the first tea bushes having sprung from the eyelashes of a monk in China. In the feature, we are introduced to a nutritionist, tea scientist and tea board chairperson talking about the benefits of tea drinking. Next, a tea planter's wife takes us through life in the tea gardens and a British journalist explains how the British made tea drinking a habit since they had tea from India, and sugar from Jamaica and some other colonies. We also hear a fascinating account from the India Office library in London of how the British bribed the tribal chiefs in Assam with rum and opium to get tea bushes from them. Finally, columnists and broadcasters Jug Suraiya and Amita Malik recount their 'chai stories'.

The feature begins with chirping birds and has a jingle with rock beats, a Hindi film song and an English song with a lilting melody, all of which stay with us for a long time. Additionally, there are various musical pieces between narratives and of course, the mellifluous voice of Indrani Roy Misra binding the show together with her smooth anchoring.

We try to keep track of the different sound formats used in it but give up halfway through, because the lure of closing our eyes and listening to the smoothly moving story is too much to resist.

We lose ourselves in the experience and Basudha looks at us triumphantly when it ends. She has made a point. The radio feature wins hands down.

'Music is an integral part of every feature,' explains Dr Ashok Srivastava, who produces Hindi features for the central unit and shares a room with Manoj Atri.

We have noticed that the types of music pieces used in a magazine and a feature differ. Ashok is a plumpish man in his fifties who uses his psychology doctorate to explain why.

He tells us that in a feature, the music piece allows the listeners to think about what was said before while moving smoothly on to the next point on the same topic. However, music is a changeover between two unrelated issues in a magazine. Therefore, the function of the music piece in a magazine is not to let the listener dive too deep into the given topic but to prepare her for a different issue altogether.

The creative use of the musical sound bites and the background sounds in a feature take away from the monotony that a mere bombardment of facts would entail. Insertion of small skits gets the same results and all producers agree that they speed up the feature and increase retention. The skit may be a minute or two long or just a sentence in the middle of a narrative. For example, Ashok inserted just one sentence by Gandhi himself in a feature on Raj Ghat, the memorial to him and the Gandhi Museum near it. It added a terrific punch to the feature, brought Gandhi into focus and made the listener's identification with the venue complete.

A noticeable element in the feature is always the catchy title, which whets curiosity and attracts listeners. A standard topic like Indo-Russian relations, on which Ashok's unit produced a feature, would usually attract only a small audience interested in diplomacy. Calling it *Volga ke Neer se Ganga ke Teer Tak* also attracted the lay audience. Indo-Russian music and references to the popularity of Raj Kapoor movies in Russia made the feature more interesting and kept the lay listener hooked. A feature on cybercrime was similarly titled *Zara Hatke Zara Bachke, Ye Hai Cyber Meri Jaan*, parodying the old popular film song filmed on Johnny Walker, the comedian.

The music pieces, songs and sounds used in the features and magazines are mostly taken from archives in AIR, which has almost every known sound required in a broadcast. Some are also taken from YouTube but kept below thirty seconds to ensure no copyright violations can occur.

'Are all these from the internet?' we naively ask Basudha, referring to the sounds in the archives, completely forgetting that radio preceded the internet by a long, long time.

'Melville recorded many of them when on assignment,' she smiles and educates us.

She shows us a register from his times. It has entries like a field gun firing, a river in spate, a Kolkata marketplace, birds chirping, tigers roaring and even the sound inside a submarine! They were all sounds recorded live, which shows the sheer amount of travelling he must have done and thus created the resources available to AIR for producing exemplary work.

From the National to the Asian Broadcasting Union award, the numerous awards won by the unit are ample testimony to its creativity.

We ask both of them about their freedom in choosing the topics for the features. They tell us the producer has the last word in at least ten of the twelve features broadcast annually. In the other one or two, the ministries may sometimes suggest topics based on some crucial landmark achievement of the government or milestones in the lives of celebrities, but leave the treatment to the producer.

We know we want to listen to a few features and magazines and we request that Basudha send us links to YouTube posts.

As we leave, our phones ping. Basudha and Ashok have sent us the requested links. The sheer breadth of the topics covered astonishes us. The discussion on the radio magazines scheduled for the next day beckons and promises to be just as enjoyable.

'I don't get any fanmail and there is no live feedback. Also, there is no revenue potential. People often ask me if anyone listens to the programmes I produce,' says Manoj Atri. 'I, however, keep going purely out of passion because I know someone out there needs these programmes and benefits from them.'

'I once did a programme on camel's milk in which we had a nutritionist and a doctor explaining the benefits of regularly consuming it. The morning after we broadcast the programme, I got a call from Lucknow profusely thanking me for it. The caller said he suffered from a disease that was causing him to lose his eyesight and from hearing the programme, he learnt that the milk of a camel contained some minerals which were just right for controlling its onset. He told me he had already ordered the milk and would start consuming it the next day but wanted to thank me before beginning to do so. Now tell me, would I crave social media's "likes" after this?' he asks with a smile.

Manoj tells us about the four thirty-minute Hindi radio magazines he produces.

The magazines, each of which plays out one Wednesday a month, are called *Sahitya Bharati*, *Sanskriti Bharati*, *Vigyan Bharati* and *Yuva Bharati*. These feature topics on literature, culture, science and things of interest to the young. Each issue is covered for two to seven minutes and includes interviews, expert opinions, music, background sounds and an anchor weaving the same into a coherent narrative.

An average magazine has between three and ten separate topics covered, depending on the nature of the topic under discussion. For example, a discussion about an author who is not so well-known nationally could extend for up to seven or eight minutes, since it takes about two minutes or slightly more for a listener to develop an interest in the topic and then a few minutes to understand it. But there can be many smaller bytes about events nationwide in a culture magazine. Similarly, the magazine for the youth could have more music than the literary magazine and may even have small skits to make a point. Music is also prominent between topics and sometimes as a part of it.

To explain what a magazine sounds like, Manoj switches on his radio, broadcasting the literary magazine of the day. The first segment has the anchor introducing a Hindi writer from Bihar, Shiv Poojan Sahai. Next, he talks about Sahai's works and then brings in the author's son, who talks about his father. A professor follows with a critique of Sahai's style and the anchor then wraps up the discussion and introduces the next topic. Thus, in under ten minutes, we get introduced to an author we would never have heard about, otherwise.

'You do this for topics as diverse as literature, culture and science?' we ask him.

'Yes,' he replies, 'when I was editing the portion on Sahai, my mind was on the bytes on nanotechnology that were supposed to come in that day but had not.'

Manoj explains that this involves keeping his eyes and ears open for anything new happening in the fields covered by his magazines. He simultaneously keeps an eye on a scientific conference in Chennai and a celebration of a festival in Arunachal while looking for topics of interest to the youth and information on authors and poets.

We ask him if his not being an expert on either of these, except by experience, makes it a daunting task for him.

'It helps me,' he says. 'Had I been an expert in either of these fields, my preconceived notions and prejudices would have clouded my point of view. Instead, as a non-expert, I can look at topics dispassionately and choose, based solely on whether it will likely add value to the listeners.'

After deciding upon a topic, Manoj researches it. He then identifies an expert who could speak on it and tells the radio station within whose jurisdiction the expert resides to get a sound bite. Next comes the editing, in which he weaves the information into a narrative, adds some music and makes the piece ready to air. It looks easy on paper, but coordinating with six to eight people scattered all over the country weekly, re-recording pieces if they don't meet the requirements, is undoubtedly daunting. In addition, policy demands that programmes be ready three months in advance and sometimes have to be changed if the external environment changes, which adds to the complication.

With the number of people contributing sound bites being large, with as many as ten to fifteen people being part of one magazine, AIR follows a strict protocol for paying them. Experts recording in the studios get remunerated and the others do gratis.

'This must require your persuasion skills to be good?' we ask Manoj.

'Some do it for the love of the topic, others for being on the radio. The only thing I am sure of is that no one refuses when we approach them.'

While Manoj talks to us, his phone rings. His face lights up as he listens to the caller and then he puts his phone on speakerphone mode for us to listen in. A farmer from Madhya Pradesh says that his daughter has just cleared the state civil services examination. He excitedly tells Manoj that her being an avid listener of the magazine programmes on AIR contributed tremendously to making her aware of many diverse topics.

'This is the objective of public service broadcasting,' Manoj says as he disconnects the call, after accepting the profuse thanks from the caller. 'And this is why I do what I do.'

No mention of the mixed format can be complete without the mention of Yuvavani. With the youth channel Yuvavani launching in Delhi, Calcutta and Srinagar in 1969, Western music presentation took a quantum leap with a phalanx of stars like Sunit Tandon, Lillete Dubey, Raman Bhanot, Sitaram Yechury and Siddhartha Basu being born to it. At this time, Delhi D station hosted Yuvavani and played a lot of pop, rock, jazz, etc. It was both a youth hangout and training ground. In its glory years, the trinity of Rita Mukherjee, Avik Ghosh and Noreen Naqvi managed the channel. Naqvi, who started as a production executive in Yuvavani, later became AIR's first female director-general.

It was a channel that had young people queuing up to participate in it and the ones who made the cut were the heroes on campus.

'Yuvavani helped popularize all Western music genres amongst the Indian listeners,' says Sunil Gupta, one-time RJ with Yuvavani, with many popular programmes under his belt in the '70s including the very popular *A Date with You* and *Forces Request*. 'My being the RJ or compere, as I was then called, ensured that I did not have to spend a single weekend without a date while at college,' says the advertising consultant, now in his sixties and reincarnated as a cricket commentator.

Though primarily a music channel, many popular non-music programmes aired on Yuvavani. Campus reporters covered all the activities on campus, including the cultural festivals, and its booth was the favourite hangout for being noticed in a college fest.

There was also a programme called *Roving Microphone*, which asked uncomfortable questions of anybody and everybody. Even during the emergency in the '70s, Yuvavani got away with broadcasting much that others were afraid even to utter.

'On *Roving Microphone*, we caught things of interest in town. We even interviewed children selling flowers at traffic lights. We asked them what they had to say about their life. Of course, they were scared to say and we were scared to ask, as, in a sense, what we were probing could reveal a critique of the government, but it opened up things,' says Rita Mukherjee. 'In *Firing Line*, we put a person at the centre of a controversy on the mat and had young people question them. So, for example, if there was a medicine scam, we could have the health minister in the studio. The idea of journalism was to make the government function so that those in power could be made accountable to the people.'

With changing listenership patterns, Yuvavani has ceased to be a channel and is an hour-long programme on FM.

For the last words on the mixed format and the spoken word, we meet Probir Sengupta, a recently retired producer from the Kolkata radio station and ask him why these excellent programmes, like features, magazines, etc., do not have the kind of listenership they deserve. We tell him about noticing that the Surajit Sen feature on YouTube had only 200 views at the time, something even a moderately connected individual can get for an uploaded video of dubious quality.

He shrugs and quotes from Thomas Gray's *Elegy Written in a Country Churchyard*.

'Full many a gem of purest ray serene,
The dark, unfathom'd caves of ocean bear:
Full many a flow'r is born to blush unseen,
And waste its sweetness on the desert air.'
'What can be done?' we ask him.

'More publicity for the programmes and concerted campaigns to increase the radio listening habit can turn the tables,' he says. 'Look at what Amitabh Bachchan has done for tourism in Gujarat with his Kuch Din Toh Guzaro Gujarat Mein campaign. Look at the awareness created by his campaign about the timely administration of polio drops. So why can't he or someone like him feature in a series of ads about radio listening? Think of him or Sachin Tendulkar holding a transistor to their ears and saying in an ad, "*Main radio sunta hoon—kya aap bhi?*" Imagine the impact it will create if the radio listening habit moves beyond the noise of FM.'

'But will it?' we ask.

He smiles a wry smile and shrugs his shoulders once more. Of course, we know this may never happen in the government setup, but what if it did?

We leave with the thought that we have another mixed format to explore before stepping into the soulful world of music—the ads and jingles on AIR.

6

The Mixed Format: Ads and Jingles

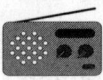

'THERE WAS A WELL IN THE REAR COURTYARD OF OUR HOUSE in Alwar. During vacations, all the children of the joint family would assemble by it in the early afternoon, draw water and splash around,' reminisces Narendra Jain, a retired IT professional, who has worked worldwide in an illustrious career spanning almost forty years. 'The actual bath would only start when our mothers would yell at us to wind up fast—and the soap we used? Lifebuoy!'

He hums the jingle, a rage when broadcast—'*Tandurusti ki raksha karta hai Lifebuoy, Lifebuoy hai jahan tandurusti hai wahan—Lifebuoy!*'

Such was the power of the jingle that when he was posted in the Middle East and would come back from field trips, all sweaty and dusty, he would find himself wishing he had a Lifebuoy to wash it off. So even to date, he uses a Lifebuoy hand wash and hand sanitizer.

The Lifebuoy ad was one of the most successful radio advertisements. It was also among the earliest since radio advertisements started in India in 1967.

The world over, though, the first radio ad broadcast was a jingle attributed to General Mills, whose catchy ditty was for '*Wheaties—the best breakfast food in the land*'. Listeners first heard it on Christmas

Eve in 1926. It initially aired only in the Minneapolis–St. Paul Market, but it was soon broadcast nationally. The resulting increase in sales established the 'Wheaties' brand nationwide, and radio became an effective advertising medium.

Other advertisers quickly saw the value in having a radio ad, particularly a custom musical melody that conveyed the name of their product more uniquely and memorably than just having an announcer say it. As a result, over the past ninety years, many influential and memorable advertising campaigns have been based around radio ads, specifically jingles.

'I agree with your friend,' says Santosh Desai, the brand guru, author, consultant and veteran adman. 'It was an iconic ad,' he smiles as he stops to hum the jingle of Lifebuoy. Then, he launches into a jingle hum medley '*Vajradanti, Vajradanti, Vicco Vajradanti*' and '*Khushboodaar antiseptic cream Boroline*'. They are still as popular.

'Do you see what was in common between them?' he asks.

'Music! Catchy music!' he answers his own question before we can reply. 'Music is a big memory trigger. It can invoke both emotion and nostalgia.'

Santosh explains that the brand's aural signature is an asset the jingle builds for the product or service. 'The repeatability of the jingle, over and over again, ad nauseam, creates a reminder which the customer will not forget easily.'

'A good jingle has a familiar sound that the brain will store and recall,' explains Kala Iyer, who has created jingles and ads for over three decades from her recording studio in Delhi. 'Likewise, if the song is annoying or disruptive, it can create a dissonance and the customer will hate your product.'

She continues, getting a little technical now, 'It's all thanks to a little thing called involuntary musical imagery (INMI). A lot of neuroscience goes into this. I'll condense what you need to know in layman's terms: when you hear a familiar piece of music, your brain floods with memories related to that tune. This is perfect for advertising your brand. Radio jingles are the only advertising method to get you hours of free airtime in your listeners' brains. They'll get stuck in their heads and when they hear bits of them again, they'll instantly remember your ad and what you told them. It's no surprise that a great radio jingle boosts brand recall so much.'

'Radio advertisements are not always jingles; many are spots,' clarifies Sujoy Sen, whose studio has produced jingles and spots for decades. He explains the difference between a spot and a jingle. 'A spot is a kind of radio drama with dialogues while a jingle is a song and much more expensive to produce.' Sujoy has produced radio dramas and hundreds of radio spots over four decades. 'While the jingle is light and frothy and is easy to remember for its catchy tune, the spot can have humour or dialogues which explain the product features,' he adds.

An advertising veteran, Rekha Nigam, concurs, 'The radio spot should make the listener "see with their ears!" The sound effects and the different voices create a sense of the visual.' She talks of a radio spot for the mosquito coil called Kachhua Chhaap. 'There was a very effective radio spot with the two veteran comedians, Mukri and Tun Tun. I don't remember the exact dialogues, but the crux was that for the suhaag raat, Mukri lifts the ghunghat and, on seeing a fat Tun Tun, shouts, "*Bachao, Bachao!*"'

The voice-over adds, '*Machharon se bachao, phir ghunghat uthao; yeh lo Kachhua Chhaap.*'

'I have forgotten the content, but the theme and the product have stayed in my mind,' she says, signifying a good spot's impact.

Says a veteran broadcaster, 'Despite radio's massive reach, the introduction of the commercial into radio had to wait till 1967. The reason was probably because AIR initially did not even broadcast film songs and the commercialization of literature and culture was anathema. So, the push for advertising and broadcasting film songs came from the same source—the Sri Lankan Broadcasting Corporation, or Radio Ceylon, as it was then called. The iconic *Binaca* (later Cibaca) *Geetmala* proved to be a game-changer.'

Later, we will talk about how the Sri Lanka Broadcasting Corporation took away listeners in droves from AIR and diverted them to the *Binaca Geetmala*, the first countdown show of Hindi film songs. It attracted listeners and did wonders for the toothpaste brand Binaca, which sponsored it. Such was the hold of the programme that when the company changed the brand name to Cibaca, it did not have to bat an eyelid to get the change across. All it had to do was change the programme's name to *Cibaca Geetmala* and people accepted the new brand name. Such was the power of radio advertising! Besides, the colossal revenue generated by the Sri Lanka Broadcasting Corporation forced the Indian government to consider launching advertising on AIR.

Though the entertainment channel Vividh Bharati, playing film music, was started in 1957, it was not till ten years later that it broadcasted its first advertisement. We ask many radio veterans if they remember the first advertisement on AIR, but no one knows.

'Recording jingles and spots was a difficult job in those days,' says Deepa Roy, a veteran voice-over artiste. She has the distinction of having recorded jingles in twenty-three Indian languages and then proceeds to explain the process.

'The technology was such that the magnetic tape we recorded had only one track and editing was impossible. The music and the vocals were, therefore, recorded together. The entire crew of musicians and singers would assemble in the studios in the morning and patiently wait for the music director to create a tune. Then, until he got it right, we would hang around, often for half a day. Once he got the tune right, the entire recording would start and even if one of the accompanists missed a beat or the singer mispronounced even one word, the whole process would start all over again. It would take a day to complete just one jingle, but the process ensured that we produced a perfect output.'

The technology has since revolutionized and the background score is recorded separately. The track of this recording is played for the singer and often with the voice of the music director singing the song along on a separate track. The lead singer follows the voice and records a jingle in as little as an hour. Most professionals have mini studio setups at home and record without knowing who the accompanists are.

'This makes the process faster,' adds Deepa, 'but it is very clinical and often, for days, I work alone with only the studio's walls for company.'

When introduced in 1967, advertising on AIR took off in a big way. Sales units were set up in major metros and sold airtime for the local and repeater stations. Each radio station had a rate list based on the popularity of the programmes and the time slots were divided into prime and non-prime slots and rates were charged accordingly. Advertising was sold in ten-second slots with a maximum of 120 seconds allowed at one time. Sponsorships for entire programmes were also sold just the way *Binaca Geetmala* was. However, with the local radio station's limited reach, rates were low and could only be sold for products with local appeal. Therefore, if an advertiser wanted to broadcast a spot or a jingle across the country, he had to submit separate proposals.

Sujoy explains that the agency had to send the script by post and get it approved. Then, they would do a demo or a rough cut and send it again. 'Twelve copies of the final version had to be prepared and sent to twelve radio stations. Getting twelve approvals was time-consuming and frustrating; many advertisers wanting a pan-Indian presence shied away from AIR.'

A Central Marketing Division was set up in Delhi in the year 2000 to overcome this and focus on revenue maximization.

Sukhjinder Kaur, our heroine of the Golden Temple episode, was given charge of it.

'When the director-general called me and asked me to take charge as the first-ever head of marketing, I was shocked. I had, after all, no experience of anything but broadcasting. He, however, insisted and I thought I would give it a try. I only asked for the staff of my choice, which was granted. Initially, we started from a small room with typical government-issue furniture and did not even have a place to call clients.'

However, this gradually changed and the marketing department got a swanky new office, rivalling the director general's, but she had to prove herself first.

'On my first day itself, I was presented with a massive challenge. The Ministry of Health had given us an advance of ₹1 crore to produce spots and promotional materials. However, we had barely started brainstorming when they asked for the amount to be returned, with interest. Since starting with a loss was not an option, I got the team together, formulated a marketing plan (despite never having made one before) and met the joint secretary who had sent the notice. He not only agreed to it but also sanctioned an extra ₹2 crore. After that, the marketing division was in business,' says Sukhjinder, who, now at seventy-five years of age, still shows the same energy and passion she had when she turned the division around.

Under Sukhjinder, the division's turnover increased from ₹75 crores a year (all India) to ₹350 crores from Delhi alone in 2018. So it is no wonder that after she superannuated in 2007, she was given one extension after another till she decided to quit in 2018.

The system operates the same way to date. The central unit handles the national or regional ad sales and the local units take those relating to that particular state. If the central team clinches a deal where the advertiser wants to broadcast only in one state, it passes the enquiry to the local sales unit.

We ask Sukhjinder why ads had to be submitted and approved before being recorded for broadcast. She tells us that public service broadcasters had a strict code of what was acceptable and what was not and all ads had to be held against that code, before being recorded.

There was, and still is, a strict no alcohol and no gutka ads policy. Also, the spots and jingles that were finally broadcast had to ensure that they did not exploit caste or religion, make fun of anyone's disabilities or encourage gender stereotyping. Obscenity or suggestiveness, double entendres, etc., were out.

'Yes, there were many restrictions on what could be advertised and how,' comments Sujoy Sen, 'but the work ethic was fantastic. If I were to use one word, I would say the advertisement broadcast had to be "clean". It was a pleasure doing business with the people at AIR who were so friendly and gentlemanly,' he adds, recalling his days with the ad agencies which dealt with AIR.

We ask Deepa Roy about the people behind the music in radio advertising.

She tells us that many famous classical musicians would record jingles in the early days of radio advertising, i.e., in the late '60s and all through the '70s, but wanted their names out of it. 'They would take payments in cash or someone else's name as they did want the money, which was not bad, but didn't want to be associated with "cheap" advertising,' she chuckles, remembering some names which she asks us to refrain from quoting.

Their presence, though, did result in some fantastic use of classical music in jingles.

'We were developing a jingle for Sargam chai and we used the words "*Subah ne chhedee hai sargam, ujiyaala chhaaya hai*",' recalls Rekha. 'A famous classical singer sang the jingle in bhatiyali dhun.'

One of this time's most endearing and iconic creations was the jingle for Bajaj scooters. '*Ye zameen, ye asmaan, hamara kal, hamara aaj, buland bharat ki buland tasveer, hamara Bajaj, hamara Bajaj*' became one of the most hummed tunes across India, thanks to radio's massive reach. It established not only the robustness of a Bajaj scooter but also its Indianness. As the scooter market opened up to foreign models, this emotional connection kept the Bajaj brand flying high—buying a Bajaj scooter was suddenly a matter of national pride. The tune was composed by Louis Banks in raag Jaijaiwanti, but unfortunately, the voices who sang the song faded into obscurity and could not make it big.

Compared to the attention-avoiding classical singers, many of today's stars from the film music fraternity and performers in light music genres like ghazal and bhajan singing started with radio advertising and proudly own up to this. Kavita Krishnamoorthy, Shankar Mahadevan, his friends Ehsaan and Loy and others like Kunal Ganjawala, Jagjit Singh, Shailendra Singh and Vinod Rathod are examples of this category.

We are intrigued that many jingle singers sing in multiple languages, with Deepa Roy singing in twenty-three! How is the translation handled, we wonder and does it not sometimes lead to glitches?

Deepa and Rekha agree that translating the jingles into local languages can sometimes be challenging. There are many bloopers when the translator does not realize that the word means something else in the local language. For example, for a paan-flavoured candy developed by Parle, the ad agency used the word 'gillori', which in Hindi meant a bunch of paans put together but meant a squirrel in some other language.

'Often, the translators do not know the original language well enough and make mistakes,' Deepa giggles. She recalls when a translator read 'khaadya' (food) as 'khaad' (fertilizer) and inserted the word 'gobar' or cow dung as the Odiya translation. It created a sentence that said that the food product advertised was cow dung.' She tells us that not being able to make sense of the sentence, she insisted on seeking clarification and understood how the blooper had occurred and corrected it. 'It is fortunate that being a Bengali and Odiya being close to Bangla as a language, I saw something wrong with the translation. Had I not been savvy to it, I would have been singing out the benefits of eating bullshit!' she bursts out laughing aloud.

A media plan for airing advertisements on radio involves first considering the audience profile of every programme and then the geographical area of demand. The timing of the usage of the product also gets due consideration.

For example, the FM Gold channel, which airs talks, discussions and magazines, always has product ads for the forty-plus age group. Similarly, Rainbow FM and pop music programmes have products for the youth, and a programme like *Sakhi Saheli* on Vividh Bharati would have products for women.

Likewise, suppose one particular part of the country has a dengue pandemic raging. In that case, the health ministry only broadcasts the ads on precautions to prevent it in that region. Similarly, advertisers of products aimed at particular areas seek ad spots on radio stations in that geographical area alone.

The timing of the usage of the product also carries weight. Rekha gives an example of the jingle for Cibaca Top toothpaste. 'There was a "ding dong" kind of music when the time check happened in the ad. Many listeners would set their watches to listen to it immediately after the time check. The words would come: *Yehi waqt hai, sahi waqt hai, Cibaca gel ka.* The ad reminded the early-morning listener that it was time for her to brush her teeth with Cibaca toothpaste. It was repeated at night. It worked wonders for the brand,' she reminisces.

'Sometimes, the positioning is also to accommodate a quirk of the advertiser. For example, we once had the maker of the Victor brand of men's briefs insist that his jingle be played on Radio

Jalandhar precisely at 7.07 p.m. every day,' she chuckles. We try to work this one out but fail to find the correlation between the wearing of briefs by men in Jalandhar and the time slot chosen for the jingle, and decide to give up looking for the yeti and join Rekha, who has by now started laughing aloud, seeing our perplexed expressions. It turns out that it was just a quirk. We ask some of our friends about their recall of old radio jingles.

'*Hawkins ki seeti baji, khushboo hi khushboo udee*' and '*Jo biwi se kare pyaar, woh Prestige se kaise kare inkaar*' for popular brands of pressure cookers is the choice of Sharad Bhansali, a retired bureaucrat and now a corporate lawyer.

Meera Johri, a publisher, remembers the Lijjat papad ads. 'Just recall *kurram karram lajjatdaar mazzedaar Lijjat papad* and you immediately imagine the crunchy papad,' she says.

Ravi Malhotra, an academic and consultant, recalls the ad for a ghee brand where the lines were: '*Paawan hai paawan, man bhaawan.*' The brand was Paawan ghee. 'Simple, straightforward and with repeat value,' he says.

'It is the music that aided their recall,' says Amit Bishnoi, who has created thousands of jingles over the past two decades. 'The music has better recall than visuals, provided it is simple, catchy and repeated well enough. My favourite is *Dhara Dhara, Shudh Dhara* … evocative yet straightforward,' he hums the jingle as he speaks.

Rekha gives an example of a catchy tune when she wrote, '*Dhoom machaa de, rang jamaa de, Pan Parag pan masala.*'

'The promoter liked the jingle so much that he instructed not to change the lines ever in future,' she says proudly.

'The simplicity of the message works so well,' Rekha continues with her examples. She recalls how they made the lines '*Soybean se bana, protein se bhara, aahaar mazedaar, Nutrella*' when developing a jingle for Nutrella soya nuggets.

Sujoy Sen points out that folk tunes are often extensively used since they ensure instant connection. He recalls a jingle for Elf engine oil for which he used the folk music of the state in which the jingle was to be broadcast. For example, in Kerala, he used the song the boat riders sang in a boat race. In Maharashtra, he used the track of a popular song sung by fisherfolk. 'It worked wonders, as people connected with it immediately,' he says, pride evident in his voice. 'We used a similar strategy for Bata Quovadis and other brands. We combined a folk tune with modern orchestration and it worked beautifully.'

Jingles have always dominated radio advertising against spots and are still used extensively in television advertising. Sunil Gupta, now an advertising consultant, recalls a campaign for Dunlop Tyres that had a conversation between a traffic policeman and a driver. Apart from the sound effects of cars screeching to a halt and other things, the two exchange funny dialogues, each ending with a description of a particular feature of the tyre.

He continues talking about how people have used the '*Bachao, bachao*' for many products. He recalls an ad by Lintas for Colgate toothpaste where a female voice shouts '*Bachao bachao*'. When a male voice sounding like a policeman enquires, the lady says, '*Har Colgate pe teen rupiye bachao.*' The ad beautifully uses the Hindi words for 'help' and 'save', which are the same—*bachao*. He adds that it instantly got a smile on the listener's face, while making the connection.

Two ads with opposing messages also stand out. In the first, the advertisement for Cadbury Chocolate Celebrations packs released in 2015 had the male voice asking about the fragrance of homemade kheer, the feel of boiling tea being served and cold water compresses being placed on the forehead when feverish—all suggestive of a mother's love. Then, after evoking nostalgia, it asked if it was possible to have these through a phone call. 'If not, then why wish your mother or aunt at the festival season on the phone,' the ad asked. 'Wish them in person'—it urged, 'and carry a Cadbury Celebrations pack.'

The other one, released in 2013, featured a conversation between a boy and the father of one of his female classmates. The father refuses to let them speak despite the boy saying he only wanted to borrow her exercise book. It ends with the voice-over asking the girl to get herself a Magic Airtel mobile phone connection to prevent her father from blocking access to her.

Yet spots, despite having caught the listeners' attention when launched, have not stuck in their minds as the jingles have.

'Unlike TV, where we can show the product, on the radio, we have to use a catchy tune and effective words to help you visualize the product,' says Sunil Gupta. 'The music helps create a sense of brand, an image and an intimacy that stays. Few things can drive an advertising message home, like a catchy jingle. Whether your listeners love or hate it, a good jingle will relate your brand name with the tune.'

The simplicity of the words and the music make radio jingles stand out. That's why we remember '*washing powder Nirma*' or the '*la la la la-la*' of the Liril girl. The phrase coined for this by Ambi Parameswaran, a doyen in the industry, is 'sound visualization'—words that are written to be heard rather than read.

'Radio is a non-intrusive medium and thus becomes very favourable for advertising. Simple lyrics and repeat value work,' adds Lakshmipati Bhatt, someone who has spent decades in advertising. He gives Godrej Storewell's example and refers to the tagline '*Saajan ki angan mein pehla kadam*' from the jingle for the iconic steel cupboard every household once aspired to own.

The standards of radio ads have plummeted lately and we are looking for a person we can talk to who can explain this to us.

We speak to Chetan Shashithal, often called the man with a thousand voices. He is a voice-over and dubbing artiste known within the ad industry for his extraordinary ability to create voices for characters and products, each different from the other. We are great fans of his work and have seen numerous videos of him performing. His ad for Closeup toothpaste, in which he introduced a jingle from the 'Kundan Lal Sehgal era', is iconic and still remembered by many. He tells us he has dubbed for over 30,000 ads or jingles and has created voices for over seventy actors and film characters. Mickey Mouse and Donald Duck to Amitabh Bachchan and Dharmendra—he has done them all. He has done ads for Center Fresh, Cadbury, Hathi Cement and many others and seems the right person to talk to about the ad and jingle industry standards.

'Why are no new campaigns creating the brand recall like those epochal radio ads of the previous times?' we ask him.

'Every ad agency in the '60s and '70s had a separate radio department that exclusively made radio ads. However, as cost-cutting pressures started bearing down upon agencies and the industry became more and more competitive, the ad agencies offloaded this function to specialized sound studios. With the introduction of an additional layer between the artistes and the clients, there were two layers of margins added on to costs and, naturally, quality suffered,' he explains.

'The studios, with lower budgets, used rank amateurs who charged less than professionals, to produce spots and jingles. A trend also emerged of taking the taglines from television spots and using them in jingles for radio. Unfortunately, those lines, having been written for a different medium, often didn't resonate with listeners on the radio. The result was substandard jingles with no possibility of attaining the standards of recall of their predecessors.' Chetan explains clearly why ads on the radio were either for the government or local businesses. The former had the money to spend on a national campaign and the latter did not mind low creativity.

Most blame the fall in standards on the advent of private FM channels. Profit maximization being the objective, they have a pressing need to garner the most listeners from limited areas against tough competition. Therefore, they cater to the lowest common denominator, charge premium rates and cut costs ruthlessly.

To survive in a ruthlessly competitive market and to attract advertisers, many FM channels often offer to create content free of charge for those buying time on their networks. Collecting the scripts from the agencies, they then get them recorded by their radio jockeys or musicians in their roles. The result is the plummeting standards of jingles and their replacement by easier and less expensive spots.

'Most of them seem to follow a template—a hammed conversation between two people—a format where any product imaginable can be introduced and the result: puerile advertising with nothing to recommend it,' says Bhatt.

'The other favourite is, of course, the Bollywood spoof. Dharmendra, Rajinikanth, Amitabh Bachchan, Sanjay Dutt, Sunny Deol and the character of Gabbar from the movie *Sholay* lend themselves easily to spoofing. Unfortunately, the spoofs suffer from being very common, done to death by standup comedians. Most are tasteless and trite, done by rank amateurs and catering to the lowest common denominator. The actor Sunny Deol was recently so upset with a caricature of him and his father Dharmendra that he sued one of the radio channels,' Chetan tells us.

Amit Bishnoi says Bollywood mimicry has its recall value and cannot be discounted, but it needs to be done tastefully. 'Mimicry is an age-old trick and works well,' he says. 'However, it cannot be an end in itself. The advertiser needs to remember that mimicry is just a tool to deliver a message. Unless the message stands out and is woven into the mimicry, giving it relevance, the mimicry remains an attention-getting gimmick that listeners soon discount.'

Chetan adds that every actor now is a brand and it is virtually impossible to mimic one without their permission, and lawsuits are common in such cases.

Sunil Gupta says radio ads can also be annoying and harm the brand or message more than the good they are meant to do. He brings us back to his favourite theme of music while agreeing with Bishnoi about the value of spots. 'But they need to weave in the music to give the recall; else, people will forget them,' he clarifies.

We ask about the future of radio advertising.

Sukhjinder Kaur tells us that many products hitherto sold on the radio were more local brands than national ones. So, we have ads for local jewellers, restaurants and businesses moving to FM radio stations or YouTube channels with local content. But she explains that AIR continues to rule the roost in the national advertising space.

She also tells us that almost 80 per cent of the ad times come from the government and the rest from the private sector. Abhijit Godbole, a veteran ad-selling professional, confirms this while stating that the ads from the government sector are at heavily discounted rates and contribute a far lesser percentage of the revenue than this statistic shows. 'How many products made by the private sector need national access?' he asks us. 'Furthermore, even for brands sold nationwide, the messages differ from area to area. Also, companies have different brands selling in various regions for most product categories. Against this, a campaign for polio eradication or encouraging voters to vote in the general election must reach every corner of the country. This is available only via AIR's massive reach,' opines Godbole.

'For a long time in the '70s and '80s, advertisers thought radio jingles in local languages were downmarket and meant for the rural class who didn't have purchasing power,' says Sunil Gupta. 'With increasing purchasing power in the hands of the large farmer, the dream listener for an advertiser on the radio would now be a farmer on a tractor, with the transistor blaring songs as he works in the fields.'

'Radio creates a sense of intimacy,' Bishnoi agrees. 'There is a degree of closeness, a personal touch, and the listener is glued to the medium. This helps to create a bond while selling the product. The jingle emerged in the medium's early days as an ideal way to impress a memorable message into the mind of an audience that could hear but not see. Radio ads, particularly jingles, still have this power and will doubtless continue to survive even in an age of new media. No one can replace the radio. It can go where no other medium can,' he says.

We could not agree more.

While jingles are music to the advertiser's ears, we turn to pure music, the classical genre—and the credit for popularizing the same goes to AIR.

7

Music: Indian Classical

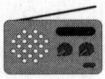

'*RAM NAAM SATYA HAI. PRABHU KA NAAM SATYA HAI,*' CHANTED the veteran broadcaster, actor and poet Harindranath Chattopadhyay. The group of musicians he led reverentially laid down the boxes they carried onto eleven biers arranged systematically on the grounds of the Lahore station of AIR.

He carried an earthen vessel, hung from hemp rope and containing burning coals, and led the radio station musicians' procession to the nearest graveyard. The words chanted by mourners at all Hindu funeral processions echoed across the roads of Shahpura as the group of mourners lamented the passing on of a dear friend.

On reaching the graveyard, they laid the boxes neatly in the graves, shovelled earth on to them and returned teary-eyed to their homes. In the boxes were eleven harmoniums, which were the property of the radio station. They were so integral to musical programmes that when their use was banned on 1 March 1940, it was as if a relative had exited their lives—hence the mourning.

The instructions, issued at the behest of Lionel Fielden, the controller of broadcasting, based on the recommendation of John Foulds, the director of Western music for AIR, banned the use of the instrument in broadcasts. His instructions asked stations not to use them as an accompaniment for classical singing and to banish them from rehearsals and even from the creation of special effects in plays and features. Moreover, the order advised the stations to auction the instruments in their custody to signify a complete break from their usage but the musicians preferred to bury their dear friends instead.

We ask Uttamrao Jule, a noted harmonium player, about the controversy. In his late eighties, Jule continues to have a childlike enthusiasm when talking about the instrument he has played for over seventy years, often accompanying greats such as Pandit Jasraj, Pandit Mani Prasad, Pandit Bhimsen Joshi and many other stalwarts.

'In Western music as in Indian, there are twelve semitones or swaras,' he explains, playing them on his harmonium, 'but in Indian music, a swara is played over a range and one swara glides into the next. Hence, a swara can be played differently in every raga. This is possible in string instruments, where the meend or gamaka lends ornamentation to a given raga or composition. In contrast, it has to be played on a keyboard instrument at a fixed place, which limits its range. This also means that those using the harmonium as an accompanying instrument can hide the lack of range in their voices,' he concludes.

He plays many solo pieces for us in quick succession. We get immersed in it and realize that the instrument's musicality is still exceptional and its appeal mesmerizing. So, while Jule seems to justify the ban on the harmonium, we root for the protestors when we leave his house.

A conspiracy theory started doing the rounds that Christian missionaries pressured the British government to ban its use as the harmonium and its pedal-operated version were derived from the church organ. Supporters of the harmonium said that the missionaries viewed a church instrument being played outside as sacrilege.

The justification offered by AIR was that this was purely a technical decision to enhance the quality of music in its broadcasts.

The ban found support from many Indians, too. Sir Raza Ali Khan, Nawab of Rampur and a great connoisseur of music, wrote that he did not consider the harmonium to be a musical instrument in the first place. Roshan Lal, more popularly known by his first name as a leading music director from Bollywood, who was employed by AIR then, came out to support the ban, though he freely used it in his compositions for Hindi films. Dr Zakir Husain, then the head of Jamia University and later president of India, wrote to support the ban, though he admitted he knew little of music. The noted musician and teacher from the Agra gharana (lineage), Pandit S.N. Ratanjankar, also supported the ban.

The most vital support came from Rabindranath Tagore. He had composed music using the harmonium extensively but, disturbed by its limitations, banned it in Santiniketan, a centre of excellence for studying and practising art in all its forms.

While AIR was considering the move, Ashoke Sen, the director of AIR Calcutta, wrote a demi-official letter to Rabindranath Tagore seeking his opinion on the proposed ban. Tagore promptly wrote back, supporting it.

'I have always been very much against the prevalent use of harmonium for purposes of accompaniment in our music and it has been banished completely from our asrama. You will be doing a great service to the cause of Indian music if you can get it abandoned from the studios of All India Radio,' the letter said.

The die was firmly cast and the instrument was summarily 'abandoned', banned and buried as in Lahore.

As the first information and broadcasting (I&B) minister, Sardar Patel did nothing to lift the ban. It continued to be enforced until 1971, with I&B ministers Dr Keskar, Dr Gopala Reddy, Satyanarayan Sinha and many others refusing to budge from the official stand. Keskar, minister for ten years from 1952, is widely thought to have banned the instrument as he was a strong advocate of maintaining the purity of Indian classical music, but the facts state otherwise.

Sporadic protests continued amongst some vocalists of the Indian classical genre, particularly those singing light classical music like bhajan, thumri, dadra, etc. However, the authorities held out against using the instrument till 1971. No one presumably wanted to bell the cat. It was left to Indira Gandhi in her stint as I&B minister to take the final decision and lift the ban.

After that, in October 1971, a few musicians like Manindra Mohan Banerjee, Muneshwar Dayal and others started using the harmonium as an accompanying instrument. However, the taboo was finally buried when, on 9 June 1974, Montu Banerjee, a staff artiste posted at AIR Calcutta, played a solo piece on the harmonium and continued to play solo compositions over time. The harmonium was back.

'When the ban was imposed, there were numerous accomplished sarangi players in the country and the sarangi is very close to the vocalist's notes. It, therefore, became the preferred instrument of accompaniment. After that, however, there was a steady decline in the quality of sarangi players. Hence, accompaniment needed another instrument and people returned to the harmonium,' T.S. Ramkumar, a veteran music producer, tells us. 'Nevertheless, its use is still not permitted during auditions for vocalists because it is believed that their true tonal quality can never be detected when accompanied by the harmonium,' he concludes.

In the early '40s, music was the most critical broadcast component and most stations devoted almost 75 per cent of their broadcast time to it. Therefore, permitting the usage of the harmonium became a hot topic for discussion in those days and continues to be discussed.

Getting established artistes to perform on the radio in the initial years wasn't easy. Part of the reluctance was because most were uncomfortable singing within a limited time. They were used to taking their own time developing the complexities of the ragas—and singing the entire raga within an hour or less, as allotted, was considered an insult to their craft. The medium also required them to be punctual and declare which raga they would sing or play at least six weeks in advance. Both were not part of their mindset because they would sing as per their moods and alter the presentation based on the audience's response.

Also, there were many misunderstandings about the technology among artistes. Patanjali Maduskar, a retired station director and someone who contributed significantly to the broadcasts of classical Indian music on AIR, tells an interesting story.

'The noted vocalist Hirabai Barodekar, when approached to sing on AIR, initially refused because someone had told her that the microphone was designed to suck her voice out of her throat. Hence, she believed that once she sang on it, she would never be able to sing without it again. In another case, well-wishers of an eminent sarangi player told him that if he sat too long in front of the microphone, it would deliver an electric shock. So, they advised him to shift his position every few minutes. So, during a performance lasting for half an hour, he got up every five or ten minutes and moved in a different direction, virtually circumambulating the microphone. No wonder he never came back,' he guffaws.

All this created a reluctance in the minds of the classical musicians and most did not perform on AIR. Also, though music schools existed, neither the number of amateurs trained nor their quality was up to the mark. Hence, that was also not a viable pool of talent to fill in the hours of programming available.

The gap then was filled by scouring the ranks of the courtesans and nautch girls from the bazaars, as they constituted the single-most significant source of trained musical talent prepared to perform anywhere for money. Many names that became nationally and internationally known because of broadcasting started their journeys from the kothas, as the dancing girls' dens were then known.

We ask all our friends in the broadcasting fraternity for the names of some of the prominent performers of that time and most tell us names but ask us not to quote them. After gaining mainstream acceptability, most made efforts to distance themselves from their origins, even changing the 'bai' (as dancing girls were addressed) attached to their names to a devi or begum.

'Some of them rose to great heights and it would be demeaning to rake up the origins of these artistes instead of appreciating their music,' says Chand Khan. He is a noted tabla player whose ancestors learned and practised their art in the same infamous lanes and by-lanes that housed kothas.

We google a few names and come up with Acchan Bai, Zohrabai Agrewali, Allah Jilai Bai, Husna Bai, Tamancha Jan, Azizan Bai, Asgari Bai, Tanno Bai and Badi Kaneez, amongst others. The quality of the music we hear blows our minds. Chand Khan tells us that some of them may not have performed live on AIR, but their vinyl records were certainly played often enough.

One name that stands out from that era is Jahanara Kajjan, a club dancer from Calcutta who had learnt Indian classical music with Ustad Husnu Khan and Western dance with Ruqayya Khatoon, another known name at that time. She danced at the European Club in Calcutta and her 'company' was sought by generals and commissioners and she was addressed as Miss Kajjan. Master Nissar, the then famous film star, picked her up from the infamous lanes of Bowbazar to star in a movie opposite him, after which there was no looking back. She went on to star and sing in many films of that time and was a regular performer on AIR.

However, the influx of the dancing girls alienated the classical musicians further, as they saw AIR as a den of disreputable women.

Efforts were made all the while to attract performing artistes to AIR. Zulfikar Ali Bukhari made great efforts in this direction when he was station director, first in Delhi and then Bombay. He worked very hard to allay the apprehensions in the minds of the musicians about appearing on AIR.

Uttamrao Jule tells us an anecdote about how Bukhari persuaded the doyen of the gharana, Ramkrishna Bua Vaze, to sing on AIR.

'In the initial years of radio, Bukhari Sahab invited Faiyaz Khan Sahab and Ramkrishna Bua Vaze to sing on AIR. While Faiyaz Khan Sahab seemed positively inclined, Ramkrishna Bua refused to sing. He said there was no way to complete a session in thirty minutes. Bukhari personally went to Bua's house and told him he would give him as much time as he wanted both in the morning and evening and asked the technical staff not to switch off the microphone until Bua asked them to. This allayed his fears and Bua agreed to be a part of AIR.'

Bukhari was unorthodox and often used innovative methods to push the cause of Indian classical music on AIR. However, a senior objected to his push for classical music during his first stint at the Bombay radio station, stating that no one listened to 'serious stuff' like this.

'He told the senior that he would prove that many people heard and appreciated classical music and asked for a day. He invited a noted vocalist of those times; his name eludes me,' says Maduskar, 'and asked him to sing raga Malkauns in the morning and raga Todi in the evening. He then called the day's announcer to his room and instructed him to announce the Malkauns as Todi and vice versa. He then told the duty officer to note the names and telephone numbers of people calling AIR to point out the error. There were five notebooks full of names and telephone numbers of people who called to point out the mistake within a day. This settled the issue once and for all and classical music was firmly in place.'

Sometimes, the musicians' egos also clashed, resulting in their non-participation. For example, in the early days, the audience response cell asked audiences to grade Hirabai Barodekar, Bai Sundarabai and Kesarbai Kerkar in order of listening preference. Hirabai was the top-ranked in that poll and Kesarbai Kerkar was third. This so miffed Kesarbai that she never sang on AIR as long as she lived. Not only this, but she did not even allow AIR to broadcast her recordings. Similarly, the sitar maestro Vilayat Khan, refused to perform on AIR, though his brother Imrat Khan was a regular.

To ensure that the musicians were given due respect, Bukhari specially instructed his staff to treat the musicians coming to perform on AIR as honoured guests. Thus, by slow persuasion, Bukhari could get some artistes within the fold of AIR. Yet, the number of classical musicians performing on AIR was still more significant in Bombay, Calcutta and Madras than in other stations. In 1947, Bukhari opted to migrate to Pakistan and became the director-general of Radio Pakistan: he is often referred to today as the father of Pakistani radio.

An exciting aspect of this era is told to us by Uttamrao Jule.

'Most of the older artistes refused to accept their remunerations through cheques. Instead, they insisted on receiving currency, preferably coins. Some of these great musicians would bring along a young boy, a son or a nephew, who could count the rupee coins reliably. It was common to see the old artiste and his young helper settle on the floor outside the studio, carefully count the money received and put it away in a little cloth bag.'

Independence saw many changes in the working of AIR. Sardar Vallabhbhai Patel took over additional charge as the I&B minister. Since he was extremely busy with the arduous task of uniting the country and persuading the local princes to sign the instruments of accession to the Indian Union, he did not have much time for this portfolio. However, he did pass a dictum that changed the face of broadcasting. In an oft-quoted phrase, he banned the participation of artistes in AIR programmes whose private life was a public scandal. 'He referred to the dancing girls whose presence as artistes on AIR was giving it a bad name. This added to the shortage caused by some artistes, mainly from north India, migrating to Pakistan.'

However, with princely states merging into the Indian Union, many musicians found themselves at a loose end as they lost the patronage of the rajas and maharajas, who could no longer afford to support them. It was a classic case of an enormous demand and a glut of supply matching each other and the musical bandwagon rolled on comfortably.

'In a way, the patronage of AIR was way better than the one given by local rulers,' says Uday Bhawalkar, the noted Dhrupad artiste. 'As it is, most local rulers were too impoverished to support musicians. Of the better off, many had tastes that lay elsewhere,' he adds, hinting at womanizing and profligacy for which some royals were known.

'Even amongst the enlightened ones who patronized musicians, the patronage was limited to the artistes the rulers personally liked. Not only this,' he goes on to say, 'the music was only as per the ruler's tastes and heard by the coterie the ruler approved of.'

The advent of AIR as a patron suddenly democratized the process. Many artistes confess in private that AIR contracts, at some stage of their careers, were their sole income source and also helped them become nationally known. While the senior artistes started getting programmes on AIR and subsequent invitations to perform all over the country, the lesser-known ones got employment as staff artistes. All this led to the creation of a musical ecosystem in which music schools started blooming.

Maduskar gives the example of Govindrao Joshi, a hugely talented disciple of Husnu Khan Sahab of Kolhapur. Not being able to support a family and learn music simultaneously, he was on the verge of giving up on his passion when a chance encounter brought him to the AIR Bombay station. He not only got to perform, but the respect accrued to him by being a 'radio artiste' got him students in Bombay and he started his classes. After that, he could divide his time between learning in Kolhapur and teaching and performing in Bombay.

Even someone as eminent as the vocalist Pandit Jasraj had no hesitation in admitting the role of AIR in making him who he was. Uttamrao Jule, who often accompanied him and his brother Pandit Maniram on the harmonium, says Pandit Jasraj frequently said, '*Shuru ke kayee saal toh hamara parivaar keval radio ke contracts par hee chalta tha bhai.* (In the initial years, my family survived on the money I got from my contracts with AIR.)'

'Pandit Jasraj was once offered a contract which he felt was compensating him for much less than he was worth and tore it up in a fit of anger,' recounts Jule. 'The then station director sat him down and said that by this act, Panditji had not only insulted AIR but the President of India on whose behalf it was offered. Pandit Jasraj was in tears and apologized profusely. He not only performed at the proposed fee, but carried the guilt with him for many years.'

The most significant fillip to the broadcast and popularization of Indian classical music on AIR was when Dr B.V. Keskar took over as the minister for information and broadcasting. He was the third and the longest-serving minister handling this portfolio, nine years and 356 days! He was highly educated, having obtained a DLitt from Sorbonne and was trained in the Dhrupad style of classical singing by Hari Narayan Mukherji of Benaras.

Some of his decisions turned out to be very controversial and many had to be withdrawn, while others were sound in theory but criticized for their implementation.

Amongst the sterling things that he began was the National Programme of Music. The first of these, in July 1952, featured a surbahar and sitar recital by Pandit Ravi Shankar. Though regular broadcasts of Indian music under the banner of 'Music of India' had been taking place since 1942, this was the first time such broadcasts were institutionalized. The programmes alternated recitals in the north Indian and Carnatic styles to have a cross-cultural understanding of musical traditions. They aired over the entire network every Saturday from 9.30 p.m. to 11.00 p.m.

He also started the Akashvani Sangeet Sammelans, in which invited artistes performed before live audiences in studios. The recordings were circulated across stations and played over the years. Keskar did this despite significant opposition from station directors, particularly those from south India who felt that the Sammelan only duplicated the functions carried out by certain non-official institutions without any advantage.

These, however, proved to be amazingly popular amongst the listeners and for many years, the passes to this programme were coveted possessions. Usha Joshi, a retired newscaster, laughs as she says, 'When the season for the Sangeet Sammelan approached and I had a call from someone who had not talked to me for years, I would know that it was for asking for passes!'

Attending a live concert gave many bragging rights, and a casual remark like, 'You know Khan sahab played Todi yesterday and I was just five feet from him. Gosh, it was heavenly,' was the done thing at parties. The Sangeet Sammelan continued without a break till 2019 when restrictions imposed by the pandemic brought it to a temporary halt, but it has since made a comeback.

'Every Sangeet Sammelan is hosted at twenty-four places. In all of them, north Indian classical music features in two-thirds and Carnatic in one-third,' informs the highly talented violin player Dr Vivek Shekhawat, a production executive at AIR. 'The schedule is planned for at least three months to ensure no raga is repeated and the balance between the north Indian and Carnatic styles is maintained. We offer a choice of three venues and three sets of accompanists from amongst the top grade artistes empanelled with us to each performer,' he says, showing us an amazingly detailed programme sheet, which impresses us deeply.

'Keskar established the Akashvani Vadya Vrinda (orchestra), which Pandit Ravi Shankar joined in 1952 as its first conductor. Twenty-seven instrumentalists from across India played together in the first-ever performance in Delhi that year. The orchestra also performed before invited audiences in major metropolitan cities and went on an all-India tour in 1956. It also had the distinction of being filmed by BBC, which played the recordings on prime-time television for British audiences,' says Shekhawat. 'Seeing Pandit Ravi Shankar stroll by, his sitar tucked under his arm, was a common sight in those days in AIR Delhi,' veteran cricket commentator Ravi Chaturvedi tells us. 'Once, in the early '70s, I walked into Akashvani Bhavan in Delhi to see Pandit Ravi Shankar waiting on the patio for his car. So I went and touched his feet and told him my name was also Ravi and he immediately came back with, "Oh, then you are also going to shine and be known worldwide."' Chaturvedi remembers that day with pride and still gets goosebumps thinking of the prophecy that came true.

'There was tremendous bonding between the artistes performing in the Vadya Vrinda,' retired producer Kamalini Dutt tells us. 'After every recording, they would have tea at a small tea stall at the rear of the AIR building. These chai (tea) sessions would go on for hours and loud laughter, ribbing, and gossiping about musicians and AIR were the order of the day. If the tea seller were still around, you could write a book with just what he had to tell you.'

The most long-lasting contribution to AIR by the Vadya Vrinda was the recording of the patriotic song 'Vande Mataram' in 1956. Contrary to common knowledge, Ravi Shankar did not compose the music but only conducted the orchestra. The composition was by one V.R. Athavale, who was on the AIR staff. He set it to tune in 1950. It continues to be played every morning just after the signature tune.

The Vadya Vrinda continues to function without a formal structure and performances are only through teams put together on an ad hoc basis for important occasions.

Another significant contribution of Keskar was the grading system for artistes, which AIR continues to implement even today. In the pre-Independence era, at Lionel Fielden's initiative, musicians of repute were recruited as production assistants in the four major radio stations to assist the station director in choosing programmes to broadcast. They were also responsible for conducting auditions for new entrants and assigning them slots. However, the process led to a lot of subjectivity creeping into selections. As a result, it led to heartburn and complaints that experts on the panel only chose musicians from the gharana or lineage to which they belonged.

Keskar standardized the selection process to address this and set up panels at the zonal and national levels. The panels consisted of six or seven experts from outside AIR, who graded artistes under four categories, with the entry-level being a B grade, the higher one B+ called 'B high', the next A, and the topmost one, 'A high'. The local panels were authorized to offer artistes grades B and 'B high', whereas, for higher grades, they were referred to the central committee. There were separate panels for north Indian classical and Carnatic music, light music, Western music and instrumental music.

Most artistes started with a B and gradually moved up the ladder, but better artistes were graded 'A high' in the first audition. The system continues and artistes carry the AIR grade as a badge of honour. For example, Uday Bhawalkar tells us he was graded 'B high' in his first audition. Dr Sangeeta Shankar tells us that her mother, the noted violinist N. Rajam, was graded as an artiste at nine years of age.

'Sometimes, the insistence on grading artistes resulted in awkward situations emerging. For example, Gopal Prashad Mishra, the guru and uncle of the khayal singers of the Benaras gharana, asked Rajan and Sajan Mishra to try their hand at performing on AIR.' We are conversing with Pandit Jairam Potdar, a noted harmonium player who often accompanied them in their concerts. 'However, when they reached the station, the director told them they couldn't perform as they were not graded AIR artistes. When asked to take an audition, they refused and did not sing on AIR for many years and finally relented when they were given the "A high grade" without an audition, based on their stature.'

'The process is still on and it is one of the fairest selection processes in the country,' Pandit Naresh Kumar Malhotra tells us. He is a vocalist of repute, a disciple of the Singh Bandhus of the Indore gharana and the producer in charge of Indian classical music at AIR. We are seated with him in the corporate-style wood-panelled conference room where the selection committee meetings happen. He shows us a compact disc received from a station for the upgradation of a nadaswaram player from B grade to B high. It contains a serial number, the current grade, the enhancement sought, the instrument's name and the pieces to be played. There is no mention of either the artiste's name or the station. The members listen to the disc, discuss and decide. In case of any difference of opinion, the chairman takes a vote and even records the dissent.

'As a result of the process, today we have almost 40,000 graded artistes and the number of the top-grade artistes is 290 for Hindustani classical and 385 for Carnatic,' Naresh tells us with a flourish. He is short and slightly balding, just a year short of retirement and passionate about his work. The energy he brings to explain his mission of keeping the flag of classical music flying is infectious.

'Have you told them about the National Awards?' asks Mukund Sharma, now the assistant director of programmes but someone who has headed the Carnatic music section at AIR for many years. He stepped into the conference room upon hearing we were there. He tells us that AIR also confers a grade above the top to senior artistes: they are, on conferment, called National Awardee artistes.

'These awards are given to those of extraordinary eminence and as of date, there are only twenty-three awardees, with luminaries such as Pandit Bhimsen Joshi and M. Balamuralikrishna amongst them. This grade is automatically awarded to artistes awarded the Padma awards by the Government of India and recipients of the Sangeet Natak Akademi awards. In addition, those who have been top-grade AIR artistes for over thirty years also get this recognition,' adds Mukund.

'We have used the grading system as one of the modes of preserving certain forms of classical music,' says Naresh. 'A prime example is the tappa, which is intricate and challenging to perform and was sung only by some leading vocalists. Names of Laxman Rao Pandit and his daughter, Vidushi Meeta Pandit, of the Gwalior gharana, Shanno Khurana of the Rampur-Sahaswan gharana, Pandit Ajoy Chakrabarty of the Patiala-Kasur gharana, come to mind. Fearing that the form would slowly die away and wanting to preserve it, we made it compulsory for artistes seeking upgradation from B to B high to sing the tappa. As a result, the tappa is learnt, taught and sung more frequently now,' he concludes as his fingers play an intricate beat on the tabletop. 'Not only that,' says Dr Vivek, 'we have preserved the playing of many instruments by creating slots for staff artistes and awarding grades to outsiders who play them. We also used their grading to invite them to perform on AIR, resulting in those musical traditions staying alive.'

He cites the sarangi to bring home the point. 'There were hardly any sarangi players left after the harmonium took over as an accompanying instrument. So, we encouraged some of the sarangi players to appear for auditions and get graded; as a result, they started getting programmes, which resulted in more people learning the instrument. So today, there are many talented sarangi players, though very few in the top grade, but I guess that will take time,' Dr Vivek says optimistically.

Mukund gives the example of A.K.J. Jose, a player of the dilruba in the Carnatic style whose entire career was salvaged thanks to the gradation by AIR. His genre was largely unknown and unrecognized, but his gradation meant he started getting concerts and students started flocking to him to learn this art form.

Mukund further adds that artistes in the classical music genre could be permitted to sing light music, but the reverse is never allowed. Naresh plays a disc on the room's excellent sound system and a nadaswaram's tones fill the space. We leave his room with his passion and the rhythm of the nadaswaram echoing equally in our minds.

'Sometimes egos of these staff artistes clashed, resulting in funny situations,' says Kamalini Dutt, a retired producer, classical dancer and storyteller extraordinaire, narrating a story told to her by her friends from AIR.

'A jaltarang (an instrument with glass or ceramic bowls filled with water at different levels and played by beating sticks against the sides of the vessels) player and a tabla player were always at loggerheads. Once, when the two players were to broadcast live together, the jaltarang player stepped out for a moment just before the programme's time for a breath of fresh air. To ruin his performance, the tabla player drank all the water from one of the vessels, thus rendering it useless for playing. When the jaltarang player returned with just two minutes to go before going live, he found the instrument had one bowl less and was, therefore, unplayable. Cries of "he drank my water" rent the studio and the performance had to be held in abeyance till he added water and tuned the instrument again.' Kamalini chuckles as she tells us this story.

'Of course, the jaltarang player got a chance to get back,' she tells us as her chuckles subside. 'During a Sangeet Sammelan, when performing live before an audience of at least a thousand, the tabla player stepped out to relieve himself and the jaltarang player "accidentally" spilt water on his drum. Both were chastised and transferred to separate stations.'

'I heard a strange and sad story from my radio counterpart while working on digitizing television archives,' says Kamalini. She talks of the person in charge of the digitizing project on AIR, who often complained that many recordings had been systematically erased from the library.

'I didn't quite believe him and wondered why anyone would erase such magnificent pieces of work. Finally, I found out the reason after just a little digging.

'From the beginning, the established policy was to appoint senior musicians to head the music sections to ensure high programme quality. This did happen, but the catch was that each would inevitably belong to a gharana. As soon as a new artiste took over the classical music section, she would first erase the music of the other gharanas stored in the library, considering it either impure or substandard. For this narrow partisan reason, hours of recordings of the country's musical heritage got lost to the next generation,' she concludes sadly.

Over a while, not only did more and more artistes perform on AIR, but they also got over their resistance to the medium and began to like it. As a result, all-time greats like Ustad Amjad Ali Khan, Pandit Shivkumar Sharma, Pandit Hariprasad Chaurasiya, Ustad Zakir Hussain, Pandit Bhimsen Joshi, Ustad Bismillah Khan and Dr N. Rajam performed regularly at the Sangeet Sammelans.

Not only did they all perform, but their attitude towards AIR changed. For example, Pandit Bhimsen Joshi, a recipient of all the civilian awards conferred by the Government of India—the Padma Shri, the Padma Bhushan, the Padma Vibhushan and then the highest, the Bharat Ratna—greatly respected the role of AIR in his musical journey. He once said, 'My gurus taught me how to sing, but AIR taught me that it was possible to sing beautifully in a limited time.'

Dr Sangeeta Shankar tells us she thought performing for AIR was very challenging. 'While performing, our attention would be on the window separating the control room from the studio. With two minutes left for the performance to end, there would be a hand signal and another one with a minute left. It was up to us to skilfully wrap up without seeming abrupt.'

Pandit Jairam Potdar laughs aloud as he tells us of the many times he, as an accompanying artiste on the harmonium, would notice the hand signals while the artiste wouldn't. 'There would be complete panic in the recording room and we would often see announcers rush into the studio and perform a silent dance miming the closing time.'

Pandit Vishwa Mohan Bhatt says, 'Though there was no live audience, the feeling that the studio's red light indicating that the broadcast was live meant that thousands were now listening. As a young artiste, it was a great high for me.'

Pandit Ram Kumar Mishra, son of the great vocalist Pandit Chhannulal Mishra and a noted tabla player, describes the feeling of ijjat associated with being on the radio. 'When the whole country hears the announcement that the next performance will be by, say, Pandit Shivkumar Sharma on the santoor accompanied by Pandit Ram Kumar Mishra on the tabla, my chest fills with pride.'

At times, radio's loss has been the gain for other audiences. R. Sundarrajan, who worked with AIR Chennai, tells us of the noted veena player S. Balachander. 'From the age of five, Balachander showed an interest in classical music and his first musical attempt was with the kanjeera, a small, circular percussion instrument. Within a year, he accompanied his brother and other musicians on the kanjeera during regular concert engagements, temple festivals, devotional congregations, etc. From age six on, his career achieved steady growth. He also learnt to play the tabla, mridangam, harmonium, bulbul tarang, dilruba and shehnai. Balachander was a fully-fledged solo concert artiste on the sitar by age twelve and it is interesting to note that he performed Carnatic music on that instrument. From age fifteen to eighteen, he served as an artiste on the staff of AIR Madras. On AIR, he played many instruments during the almost daily broadcasts. He also performed in solo recitals, participated in orchestral ensembles, accompanied other artistes and composed and conducted his pieces.'

'The hectic stint at AIR ended with the entry of the veena into his life. Falling in love with the instrument, he felt it deserved his undivided attention and left AIR to learn it. Even without a tutor or master to guide him, he was an established concert veena player within two years. He felt that "by the grace of God" he was able to bring credit to himself for his achievement of having evolved a new trend, a new style and a new school of veena-playing.'

Sundarrajan concludes, 'AIR's loss was again for the world!'

Uday Bhawalkar admits that his performances on AIR gave him national acclaim, whereas he was previously known only in the circles he sang in. 'When I performed in Sangeet Sammelans on AIR, music buffs all over the country knew me, but the day I was featured in *Sangeet Sarita*, I was a celebrity on the streets of Bombay. All my relatives, servants, my paanwaala and my washerman, almost everyone I knew, congratulated me. I got more concerts after being featured on it.'

Uday's acknowledgement of the debt of gratitude he owed to *Sangeet Sarita* makes us keen to learn more about the phenomenon.

'*Sangeet Sarita*, started in the '70s by the violinist Bhubaneshwar Mishra, is a small programme introducing Indian classical music to the lay listener. Initially, it was a ten-minute capsule. First, the announcer described the raga's nature and played a vocal or instrumental piece from the archives, then followed it up with a film song based on the raga for easy identification in the listener's mind. Bhubaneshwar compered the programme successfully till his retirement in 1983.'

'The programme had by now become extremely popular,' says Jayant Patrikar, a veteran announcer on Vividh Bharati. 'The simple commentary made it attractive for music students and lay listeners. Moreover, playing film songs based on the ragas made the programme even more relatable.' He informs us that this was broadcast before 7 a.m. and repeated in the evening.

'The beauty of the programme is that it attracts even those not learning or knowing about classical music,' says Prof. Muley, a retired sitar teacher at the Maharaja Sayajirao University, Vadodara. 'Every time a film song based on the raga plays, a simple connection gets established and the listener's attention is grabbed. Moreover, with so many classical musicians who also composed for films, like Ravi Shankar, Pannalal Ghosh, Timir Baran, Ram Narayan, Raghunath Seth, Sultan Khan and Alla Rakha, there is a lot of material to create the programme.'

After Mishra retired in 1983, the baton passed on to the charismatic Chhaya Ganguli. She was an artiste on contract with the recording label HMV and was learning ghazal singing music from the renowned Madhurani Faizabadi. In 1979, at twenty-seven, she won a National Award for her song '*Aapki Yaad Aati Rahi Raat Bhar*' for the film *Gaman*.

'It was a library-based programme when I joined and I continued with the existing format till 1985,' recalls Ganguli. 'In a meeting in Mumbai towards the beginning of 1985, Mr M.P. Lele, the then deputy director-general and a great music lover asked me why I wasn't using my extensive contacts to take the programme to the next level. His insistence set me thinking and Kabban Mirza and I, then a production assistant and announcer, set about making a list of all the people we could approach for the programme. At the end of just one week, we realized the list was so long that we could sustain the programme for years.'

When Chhaya tells us, we discover that the baritone voice announcing '*Sangeet ... Saritaaa*' is that of Kabban Mirza, who became famous for his song '*Khuda Khair Kare*' from the film *Razia Sultan*. 'He had a unique voice,' Chhaya adds.

Chhaya Ganguli, a sprightly seventy-plus who comes across as much younger and full of life, ran the programme for fourteen years until her promotion in 1989.

'I first asked for a more extended slot and the time got enhanced to fifteen minutes. Then, instead of just taking various ragas and talking about them, I explored the entire classical music genre. Also, I made the programme episodic, to increase the range of things I could handle. Besides my efforts, this would require tremendous cooperation from senior artistes and I am proud that no one refused. The result? Twelve years of fantastic programming,' she tells us.

Senior artistes often went to great lengths to be part of *Sangeet Sarita*.

'I recorded a series called *Naad-Ninaad* with Vijay Raghav Rao, the noted flautist, composer and musicologist. In fourteen episodes, he went over the evolution of music, starting from the emergence of the first swara. He recorded non-stop from eight in the morning till ten at night for four whole days for this,' Chhaya proudly tells us.

Shivkumar Sharma recorded ten episodes on the santoor. He described its use in Kashmiri folk music and its evolution into an instrument for classical performances. The noted composer, Anil Biswas, recorded twenty-six episodes of film music based on various ragas, tracing the journey from Raichand Boral of the 1920s to R.D. Burman of the 1990s.

The episode on the Maihar gharana had ITC collaborating with AIR by lending many rare recordings for the programme. Many other greats took part in the journey and converted it into a 'music appreciation course' for the masses.

'One of my fondest memories is of Ustad Zakir Hussain calling me to Pune to record one half of an episode on the tabla,' Chhaya tells us. Noticing our wonder about why that was special, she explains, 'Despite his commitments, he took out time for me. Then, he completed the recordings in Mumbai and rushed to catch a plane for the USA straight from the studio.'

The producers' sincerity, the senior artistes' support and the programme's design made it phenomenally popular. Though old episodes are now being repeated, they continue to be followed with the same enthusiasm. 'It is nutritious fast food,' is Chhaya's final take.

Sangeet Sarita could reach out to mass listeners and continue attracting them because it airs on Vividh Bharati, AIR's top-rated entertainment channel. Though broadcasting mainly film music, it caters to other genres, too. To explore it, we turn our attention to Mumbai, where the Vividh Bharati section has its headquarters.

8

Music: Vividh Bharati

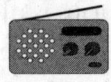

IT WAS THE '50S AND AIR WAS IN TURMOIL—IT WAS LOSING thousands of listeners daily. They were all deserting it to listen to Radio Ceylon (now Sri Lanka Broadcasting Corporation). The reason was not far to see. It was not just the excellence of Radio Ceylon that was causing it, but that it was pressing the right nerves in the listener's mind. AIR was blind to the changing tastes of its listeners.

The desertions were primarily because of AIR's decision not to play film songs. Many classical music purists within AIR had been grumbling against film music and its 'low quality' in AIR for years and questioning why AIR had to depend on film music and why a programme of light music created by AIR did not take the place of film songs.

When Dr Keskar took over as I&B minister, he acted against film music and set limits on how much it could be broadcast in a day. He ruled that film music should not, within six months of the order, constitute more than 10 per cent of the broadcast time devoted to music (15 per cent in exceptional cases) and was to be totally eliminated in eighteen months.

The order, when implemented, naturally created vacant slots to fill and AIR set up special light music production units in individual stations to create content. These units took many steps to ensure quality and offered prizes to independent producers for content creation. In addition, tie-ups were initiated with music companies for recording and releasing such content. However, all the effort came to naught as the programme did not meet the listening public's approval. They migrated to Radio Ceylon.

We dig into the history of Radio Ceylon. We discover that it is South Asia's first broadcasting station, which began operations in 1925. During the Second World War, Radio Ceylon was used by the British to counter propaganda from Japan and Germany. Early on, realizing the popularity of Indian film music both in Hindi and Tamil, Radio Ceylon started playing these songs as part of many iconic programmes. The foremost amongst them was *Binaca Geetmala*. It was a film music-based programme, started in 1952, in which, in the initial years, seven contemporary songs were played in no particular order. Soon after, pieces began to be graded, considering listener's choices and the number of records sold in the Indian market. This concept is believed to come from the American 'Top 40'.

The silken voice of the iconic Ameen Sayani saying, '*Bhaiyon aur behno, main hoon aapka dost Ameen Sayani, aur le kar aaya hoon aapka pasandida programme, Binaca Geetmala*', had the Indian listening public drooling. Arguments about which songs would make it to the top and whether the one there was deserving were often heard on street corners and in high society parties alike. The famous word on everyone's lips was 'paaydaan', used by Sayani to indicate levels. Sayani played the songs in the reverse order of their popularity from twenty, charted the movement of each piece and infused tremendous energy into announcing the climb up the paaydaan. Whether it was the format, Sayani's silky voice or the energy he invested into the programme, the fact remains that listeners thronged to it.

The loss was entirely AIR's as Radio Ceylon lapped up revenues from sponsoring Indian companies. It pinched AIR and many sections of society hard because everything about the programme was Indian. It had Indian film music, was produced by an Indian (Hamid Sayani), compered by an Indian (Ameen Sayani, Hamid's younger brother) and heard by Indians. It was even recorded in India (in the studio of the technical department of St. Xavier's College, Bombay) advertising Indian products. The listenership and the revenue, though, were going to Sri Lanka.

It was not just Hindi-speaking listeners but also the Tamil-speaking ones who flocked to Radio Ceylon. Tamil, a common language for many in Ceylon, had its own Ameen Sayani. His name was Mayilvaganam and many of the senior generation in Chennai still remember his soothing voice speaking in Jaffna Tamil.

'Mayilvaganam was very involved with Tamil stars such as Sivaji Ganesan, MGR and other famous stars; such was his pulling power on the Indian subcontinent,' Prof. M.V. Krishnamoorthy, now eighty-eight and a resident of Chennai, tells us.

'Mayilvaganam and his wife were the catalysts who brought stars like MGR and Saroja Devi to Sri Lanka on their first visit in October 1965. They came to judge a beauty pageant in Kandy, sponsored by Independent Newspapers Ltd. My father recalls the day MGR and Saroja Devi visited Mayilvaganam's residence in Colombo. The railway tracks, streets and beaches were spilling with crowds shouting and screaming to see the stars,' adds Suresh Subramaniam, a retired travel guide in Colombo.

Such was the popularity of Radio Ceylon that the broadcaster had to announce 'Ceylon Radio does not indulge in politics' when Indian newspapers spread a rumour that candidates contesting for the elections in India in 1957 could campaign on it.

Meanwhile, in India, people were out in the streets demanding an entertainment-based programme on AIR. This found an echo in the Parliament, too. On 7 April 1954, Harindranath Chattopadhyay, a broadcasting veteran and film actor, then a member of the Lok Sabha, launched a scathing attack, criticized the functioning of AIR. He argued that the government should allow film and popular music.

The thought began to crystallize in the ministry and, bowing to public pressure, Dr Keskar agreed to the demands. As a result, the newly formed entertainment channel called the 'All India Variety Programme' began broadcasting on 3 October 1957.

This broadcast began with a song penned by Pandit Narendra Sharma, the noted poet and film lyricist, sung by the famous playback singer Manna Dey and set to music by Anil Biswas. The song '*Naach Re Mayura*' became very popular on Vividh Bharati and later, HMV included it in their album during the rainy season. The lyrics symbolizing the successful culmination of a dream becoming a reality were apt for the occasion. In the song, Sharma compares the happiness at Vividh Bharati's launch with the joy a dancing peacock feels in the rainy season.

He had reason to feel joyful at the launch since he had played a significant role in conceptualizing the channel. He was the Hindi advisor to Jawaharlal Nehru, the then Prime Minister, and it was rumoured that Nehru himself had asked Sharma to create such a channel.

The announcement '*Ye Akashvani ka panchrangi karyakram hai*' started the broadcast many years ago. The announcement's wording stated its intent to have film music plus a programme featuring other arts like painting, sculpture, theatre, etc. Whereas other art forms featured in Vividh Bharati eventually got edged out by film music.

A few words by Maithili Sharan Gupt, designated by people as the rashtra kavi, preceded the first announcement. He said:

'Manas bhavan mein aryajan jiski utaare aarti
Bhagwan Bharatvarsh mein gunje humari Bharati.'
(In the temple of the mind, people worship the Lord
In India, our language echoes.)

He took the lines from his epic poem *Bharat Bharati*. It was probably taking a cue from these lines that Pandit Narendra Sharma suggested that the channel be called Vividh Bharati. If the word Bharati were taken to mean India, it would mean the diversity of India.

Kamal Sharma, the star announcer of yesteryear, recalls asking Narendra Sharma about the thinking behind the name. 'He told me Akashvani had many programmes for intellectuals, but there were none for those listeners whom he, for lack of a better phrase, called lay listeners. These listeners were looking for a variety coupled with Indianness, so with them in mind, the phrase Vividh Bharati was coined.'

While Vividh Bharati started gaining ground, things were not going well for Radio Ceylon. One of the reasons was political.

With the rise of Dravidian parties in Tamil Nadu in the 1970s, the demand for a separate Tamil Eelam gained ground in northern Sri Lanka. With the increase of the insurgency and a feeling amongst the majority Sinhala population that India was backing the demand, fault lines emerged between Ceylon broadcasters and Indian listeners. As a result, on 14 August 1970, Radio Ceylon announced that they would progressively reduce and stop playing south Indian film music. Sinhala listeners objected to Tamil film songs serving as propaganda for the DMK party, which won the elections in 1967 and in the process, fuelled the aspirations of the Lankan Tamils. As per the weekly *Sutantarian*, published by the Federal Party of Tamils, the songs of Tamil poet Subramania Bharati were also banned as the lines went something like 'we will build a bridge across the sea (to Ceylon)', which was making the Lankan authorities very uncomfortable.

Soon, all programmes except the *Binaca Geetmala* ceased to air on Radio Ceylon. (It moved to Vividh Bharati later in 1989 and continued till 1994.)

Radio Ceylon's loss was Vividh Bharati's gain and it was time for Vividh Bharati to emerge into its full-fledged avatar.

'On 3 October 1957 at 10.13 a.m., the Bombay and Madras stations started relaying Vividh Bharati on shortwave 19- and 25-metre bands. Bombay was for the north and west of India, while Madras was for listeners in the east and south. Sheel Verma was the first announcer on Bombay and Rajlakshmi on the Madras station,' says Patanjali Maduskar.

'The place in the history books for being the first announcer on Vividh Bharati, Madras, came to Rajlakshmi purely by default. The day the first programme was to be aired, the regular announcer took off for personal reasons and instantly needed a replacement. Though Telugu-speaking, Rajlakshmi knew Tamil and was the only one available. She went on to be a much-loved announcer on the channel for seven years after that,' tells Maduskar. 'Initially, Vividh Bharati broadcast pre-recorded programmes and they were all created in the Central Production Unit and sent across to the broadcasting stations.'

We chat with Yunus Khan, radio jockey at Vividh Bharati, author, poet and blogger. He and his spouse, Mamta Singh, also a broadcaster on AIR, can be called the first couple of Vividh Bharati today.

'After we recorded the programme, copies were made for the stations airing them. Vividh Bharati obtained special permission from the recording companies to copy their songs on to tape for a one-time broadcast. There was a regular carpentry section in the station for making wooden crates, and the tapes were packed in these and sent off through the postal department to the stations. I joined in the '90s and today, I am one of the few still in service who have seen that phase,' says Yunus, recalling the early days.

'By post? But that would take a long time. So how did AIR ensure broadcasting stations got the tapes in time for a simultaneous broadcast?' we ask him.

'We normally took a forty-day lead time, which accounted for mishaps and delays. We would often record three or four programmes in advance and keep them ready.' The excitement of the times is evident on Yunus's face as he recalls the early days of coordination, which were stressful yet enjoyable.

He adds, 'At the outset, ensuring listeners connected to the newly launched channel was necessary. Therefore, taking a cue from Radio Ceylon, a programme called *Patravali* started on day one. It served both as a feedback mechanism and a rapport-building one. Listeners would take pride in having their letters included in the programme and often complain of neglect if they were not.'

'I have written you three letters and you have not included even one in the programme. Are you angry with me?' was a common refrain. We laugh aloud as Jitendra Maitryana, a senior announcer on Vividh Bharati, tells us about the listeners.

'You didn't even know them and they were one of the thousands who heard you; did such letters annoy you?' we ask him.

'For the announcer, a listener is one amongst thousands, but for the listener, the announcer is a voice that enters his house every day and is part of his existence. The illusion of intimacy that the announcer's voice creates is real for the listener and hence the letters show the depth of the connection we established,' says Maitryana. He is a tall, slim man in his mid-fifties whose voice completely belies his age.

'In the initial days, Vividh Bharati wrote letters to its listeners explaining what the channel proposed to do and invited their comments. We thought we would need at least a month to mobilize our listeners, but we were flooded with letters within a week—the emotional connect was firmly in place,' he concludes with pride dripping from every word spoken.

Of all the iconic programmes broadcast on AIR, the credit for being the longest without any format change rests with *Hawa Mahal*, about which we had heard before while talking of plays on radio. It first aired on 20 October 1957 and has been broadcast almost non-stop. *Hawa Mahal* features a fifteen-minute skit every day, primarily a satire or a comedy. Each evening, millions of listeners listen to the radio plays which have held them in thrall for years. The first episode of *Hawa Mahal* was a musical play written by Pandit Narendra Sharma. Skits, anecdotes and stories continue to be written or adapted for this programme.

Vividh Bharati has been known for catchy signature tunes for its programmes and *Hawa Mahal*'s is no exception. 'The signature tune was first composed by Pandit Satyendra Sharath based on a Gujarati song, but later, he composed a fresh one in 1960, which is still in use,' Jitendra informs us.

'Play the signature tune to a million people in the age group thirty and above and ask them what it is. At least 90 per cent will recognize the tune as being of *Hawa Mahal*.' Thus speaks adman and consumer behaviour researcher Chandramouli, talking to us about the brand identification of this tune when we ask him about the significance of signature tunes.

'Not only that, but they will also immediately recall their time spent listening to the plays, transistor in hand, while enjoying their dinner or relaxing on the charpoy in the open, below the stars,' he adds. He recalls the countless nights spent in rural India observing consumer behaviour in the '70s and '80s and being connected to the outside world only through the transistor radio.

'*Hawa Mahal*, despite being just a short fifteen-minute programme, engages the listeners very effectively. It is a huge revenue earner for Vividh Bharati and spots got booked up to six months in advance,' says Sukhjinder Kaur, the retired head of marketing for AIR.

'Everything about Vividh Bharati in those days had class stamped on it. The iconic signature tunes of most programmes were composed by greats like Anil Biswas, T.K. Jayarama Iyer, Emani Sankara Sastry, Suryakumar Pal, Krishna Bhattacharya and Ninu Majumdar and the programme was created and compered by legends,' reminisces Kamal Sharma, a veteran announcer.

Sharma recalls personalities like Madhup Sharma, the interviewer turned actor and lyricist, Shaukat Kaifi, wife of Kaifi Azmi, the famous lyricist and Urdu poet Rifat Sarosh, and writer Satyendra Sharat as stars on Vividh Bharati. From the beginning, Shaukat was associated with the renowned programme *Manchahe Geet*, while Satyendra Sharat was responsible for *Hawa Mahal*. Due to his background as a poet, Rifat Sarosh presented songs and ghazals in a programme called *Gajra*.

Yunus says, giving a bit of history of Vividh Bharati, 'The studios then were located in barracks where the new building for AIR stands in Worli. For some reasons that were never clear, the service was shifted to Delhi in 1958. A significant change after the shift was that a "Carnatic Sangeet Sabha" was started. Film, folk and classical music in Tamil, Telugu, Kannada and Malayalam were also aired on Vividh Bharati with a ninety-minute slot allotted daily. Vividh Bharati continued to function from Delhi till 1972, whence it shifted back to Bombay into its new building in Borivali. Possibly, the transition was due to the realization that with the Hindi film industry being in Bombay, any programme relying on it for content had to be as close to it as possible.'

When we mention the unchanged formats of a programme like *Hawa Mahal* and *Sangeet Sarita* to Jayant Patrikar, he agrees that most structures have not changed, which is a testimonial to their popularity. He adds that even the sequence of programmes has remained constant for many years.

'Vividh Bharati wakes people today with a few chaupais (couplets) from the *Ramcharitmanas*,' says Patrikar. '*Vandan Waar*, a programme of devotional music, follows this. But it is *Sangeet Sarita*, the programme immortalized by Chhaya Ganguli, which thousands of music lovers look forward to each morning at 6.45.'

We mention Chhaya telling us of Kabban's voice announcing the *Sangeet Sarita* programme. Patrikar adds, 'Incidentally, not many people know that Kabban Mirza used to work as a radio announcer with Vividh Bharati in Mumbai. In his programme, *Chhaya Geet*, many listeners recall his distinct voice announcing, '*Chhaya Geet sunne walo ko Kabban Mirza ka aadaab.*'

Maitryana explains that each programme has a theme or common strain. The songs played at different times are categorized well, allowing the listener to choose their timing based on their preferences.

He explains: 'For instance, *Bhule Bisre Geet* has music from films between 1932 to 1955, the programme S*ada Bahar Nagme*, aired in the afternoon, has songs from the '50s onwards. Similarly, *Shyam Sindoori* has pieces from the '70s and '80s, while non-film songs are aired in *Rangawali*. The latest film songs are played in *Chitralok*, there is another slot for non-film ghazals called *Guldasta* on Tuesdays, while pop music is played on Thursdays in *Pop Express*. During the day, there is also some repetition of the older recorded programmes.'

Privately owned FM channels also play film music, but Vividh Bharati stands out because the content is not specific to one genre or period and excels in comparison. We have heard of the periods covered and genres broadcast and now turn to look at the quality of the compering.

Another senior executive from a private channel who doesn't want to be named says, 'The fixed slots for Vividh Bharati programmes are a great plus and convenience. The listeners know when to tune in to their favourite programme. This makes some of their programmes timeless and iconic in the true sense. People have built their routines around them.'

Talking of routine, Kunal Sen, a listener of AIR from Kolkata, adds, 'My father set his watch listening to AIR. And he would sit down for the meal precisely at 1 p.m. when Barun Haldar would be delivering the news.'

The time slots are also meaningful for most programmes. 'The beauty of the Vividh Bharati programmes is targeting the specific segment,' concurs Harbinder Singh Gill, owner of a fleet of trucks in Alwar, Rajasthan. 'My drivers like a phone-in programme called *Dekho Magar Pyaar Se*, which is meant for drivers of commercial vehicles. It airs at 1 a.m. when they feel drowsy while driving at night.'

'There is much more grace and dignity in the compering at Vividh Bharati as against the senseless prattle on the private channels,' says Devyani Paramanand. She is in her mid-forties, a chartered accountant by qualification and an artiste and aesthete by choice. An avid Vividh Bharati listener, she wonders why private FM channels cater to the lowest common denominator despite the freedom to do anything.

'Some of the presenters on FM channels are good, but they form a small percentage,' she says. 'Most of the time, it is poor content and presentation. If either were good, those channels would be worth listening to, but as they stand, I challenge you to talk to a hundred people from diverse age groups and ask them if they have ever heard a private FM channel for two hours continuously. If you find such a person, please introduce them to me because I have yet to find one,' she concludes.

We understand that this reaction is typically from the age group Devyani belongs to, which does not appreciate the latest music and the fast-paced style of talking of the RJs of the private FM channels.

Though there is an audience for the style adopted by the private RJs and the music played by them, we understand that those holding the opposite view also form a sizeable segment and convey our appreciation to Yunus and Maitryana.

They tell us that they are trained at Vividh Bharati to announce the names of the movie, singer, lyricist and music director while presenting a song, which ensures all of them get equal credit for the creation. We remember reading that the noted lyricist Shailendra, responsible for penning many Hindi film hit songs, once said Vividh Bharati was why he became a household name.

'We always try to add value to the listener by telling them facts they may not know,' says Jitendra.

He talks about the programme *Kuch Baatein Kuch Geet*, which broadcasts at 1 p.m. 'In this programme, the presenter decides the topic and chooses the songs woven around the theme. For example, I once gave titbits on the *Rashtriya Krida Diwas* about how the famous cricketer Salim Durrani was the first to act in a film. On another occasion, I discovered that the character actor Jankidas, who some people may know as an Olympian cyclist, was also selected for short put and javelin throw but couldn't go for the same. I mentioned that in my talk.'

'At one time on the first of every month, Vividh Bharati would play the song "*Aaj Pehli Tareek Hai*" and people looked forward to it,' says Yunus. 'Qamar Jalalabadi wrote it and Sudhir Phadke set it to music.'

'Creature of habit?' we tease him. 'Even in a normal conversation, you cannot name a song without mentioning the lyricist, singer and music director!' All of us laugh out loud.

Jitendra tells us of a programme *Aaj ke Fankar*, specific to a particular artiste, a music director, lyricist, singer or anyone else in the film industry. 'He informs listeners that the episodes are aired on their death or birth anniversary to make them more meaningful.'

We ask about the listeners' choice programme and names tumble out—*Manchahe Geet*, *Aapki Farmaish*, *Hello Farmaish*, *Hello Saheli* and the extremely popular *SMS ke Bahane VBS ke Tarane*. The last was a live SMS-based programme, which was later converted to a letter-based one and was immensely popular.

Every Vividh Bharati announcer has stories about the listeners' choice programme. For example, Lokendra Sharma, the veteran broadcaster looked up to by almost every radio staffer and often consulted by Vividh Bharati staffers even a decade after his retirement, tells us that his first broadcast was compering *Manchahe Geet*. The slim-framed, white-bearded Sharma looks every inch the benevolent family elder he is revered as. He is charming and even invites us to stay with him when we visit Mumbai next. His mellifluous voice is impressive, but he insists it is not a patch on what it was during his heyday.

'I was a total rookie, had just been appointed and did not get an assignment for the first few days. So I asked Pandit Narendra Sharma, then the chief producer, to give me one. He got up, asked me to follow him to a studio, put me in front of the microphone and handed me a script. The red light came on before I knew what was happening and I was broadcasting live. The programme was *Manchahe Geet*, the most popular listeners' choice programme. Until it was discontinued during the pandemic, the format stayed the same,' Lokendra Sharma recounts.

'Those were the days listeners wrote letters to us, mostly postcards,' says Yunus, 'and when they came in every day, it was as if there were a deluge. The post office catering to Vividh Bharati reserved a van to send the five stacks of letters we received daily. The postmen hated our beat because they had to haul those sacks to our fourth floor offices daily!' He laughs out loud as he recounts past incidents.

Yunus explains the process: 'The letters went to a sorting department exactly like the sorting unit in the post office. First, each letter went into the cubbyhole designated for the programme it was meant for. Then, the bunch went to the production assistant for that programme, who read them and decided which ones to include in the day's broadcast. The assistants ensured that all the centres from which letters came were represented and that no one person got his choice repeated too often. These chosen letters then went to a typist who incorporated the names and their preferences in the script, which we heard on the radio. Vividh Bharati currently employs fifty to sixty full-time staffers at the Central Production Unit, but at that time, at least half this number sorted out the letters received.'

'Were there any places which tended to send letters more often than others?' we ask Yunus.

'Though letters came from all parts of India, some areas had prolific writers and communities. For example, Itarsi in Madhya Pradesh, Mohali in Punjab, Khandwa in Madhya Pradesh, Bhataparain Chhattisgarh and an area of Delhi called Majnu ka Tilla had the most letter writers. But, of course, Jhumri Telaiya was the real champion.'

We ask him to tell us more about the town whose primary claim to fame was that its residents wrote letters requesting songs in listeners' choice programmes in Vividh Bharati.

As expected, Yunus feeds our curiosity and is ready with trivia and titbits, making for exciting listening. He tells us, 'Many believed for long that such a place did not exist but was made up by the radio announcers till a series of newspaper and magazine articles in the late '70s established its bona fide existence in the minds of the listening public. The identification of Jhumri Telaiya with Hindi film music through Vividh Bharati was so strong that the town found mention in several movie dialogues and songs. An example is a movie called *Mounto* (1975) in which Saira Bano danced to the song "*Main Toh Jhumri Telaiya Se Aayi Hoon*" as she diverted the villain's henchmen to enable the hero to enter his hideout. As recently as 2017, Ranbir Kapoor sang "*Mera Gaon Jhumri Telaiya Hai*" while wooing Katrina Kaif.'

We look at a map in Yunus's office to find that it is a small town in Jharkhand, which became prominent when the British discovered mica in the area while laying a railway line in the 1890s and developed mines. It derives its name from the original village Jhumri (the name of a local folk dance) and Telaiya, which means a small lake.

'The lake was formed by the dam erected near it,' reminisces Richa Chabra, a school teacher in Vadodara who stayed in the town in (then) Bihar in her childhood. 'However, the reason for it getting so well known throughout India was neither the mica extracts strewn through the dusty road surfaces nor the dam, but its close connection to the listeners' choice programme on radio.'

She continues, 'Sending song requests started with a famous mica tycoon, Rameshwar Prasad, who sent twenty to twenty-five song requests even in the Radio Ceylon era. The trend caught on when paan-shop owner Ganga Prasad Magadhiya and electronics shop owner Nandlal Sinha started doing the same. Spreading like wildfire in no time, what began as a pastime became a cult. Clubs formed to listen to songs collectively and competitions started as to who could send the maximum song requests in a day or a month.'

She pauses and chuckles as she remembers that some clubs bribed mail carriers so that their letters got a better chance of getting sent to the radio stations.

She recollects her father telling her about one Modiji who would hold meetings at Jhanda Chowk to discuss the song to request next. His acolytes would gather around him and Modiji would warn them, '*Aisa waisa gaana nahi farmaish kar sakte, Telaiya ka ijjat ka baat hai.* (We cannot ask for just any song, it is a matter of the prestige of Jhumri Telaiya.)' Richa mimics her father in a typical Bihari accent and we laugh.

A programme very close to the heart of Vividh Bharati and the Indian film industry is the listeners' choice programme called *Jaimala* and its spinoff, *Vishesh Jaimala*. They featured songs requested by the members of the Indian armed forces.

'At the time of Chinese aggression in 1962, the whole nation was in turmoil because it was the first time since Independence that a foreign power had attacked us,' says Lokendra Sharma. 'A strong undercurrent of patriotism was flowing through the country to which Vividh Bharati was no exception. Against this backdrop, the chief producer, Narendra Sharma, decided to launch a unique programme that would cater to playing songs requested by the members of the armed forces. It was aptly titled *Jaimala* as a garland of victory presented by Vividh Bharati to our soldiers.'

'In the initial years, it was customary only to have female announcers host the programme,' continues Sharma. 'Probably because it was thought that a female voice would help the soldiers on the border recall their own families, but I am not sure. As a policy, no sad songs were played on the programme because the idea of the programme was to lift the soldier's morale.'

'*Jaimala* was my favourite programme,' recalls Colonel (retired) Vikram Pande, who looked forward to the programme when posted as a young officer in J&K in the mid-1980s. 'The broadcast timing suited us very well,' says Col Pande. 'After 7 p.m., the fauji is free as he has finished his evening games or PT and is waiting for dinner in the langar. So this is the time the programme came on with his favourite songs.' Pande recalls writing many postcards to AIR and encouraging his troops to do the same.' And the excitement when the announcer announced the names of the soldiers sent a wave of cheer in the barracks,' he reminisces.

One of the spinoffs of *Jaimala* was a programme called *Jaimala Sandesh*, which was aired on Saturdays. In this programme, the families of the soldiers wrote messages to them and sent them to Vividh Bharati, which the announcers read out. The programme went on to be a big hit amongst the soldiers and their families.

In 1965, Pandit Narendra Sharma started another spinoff that overtook even the original *Jaimala* programme in popularity. In this, notable personalities from the film fraternity presented the *Jaimala* programme every Sunday, discussing their experiences and playing songs. The famous actor Nargis presented the first *Vishesh Jaimala* programme and Lokendra Sharma assisted her.

'In those days, we worked in pairs with one announcer and one assistant, forming a team in all the programmes on Vividh Bharati. The announcer would do the compering and the assistant, called the effects man, would play the records. In the case of *Vishesh Jaimala*, both roles were always allotted to the announcers to ensure there were no mistakes. So when Nargisji flew in to present the first *Vishesh Jaimala*, I had the honour of proudly sitting across her and playing the records,' recounts Lokendra Sharma.

Then began a series in which many prominent film personalities presented episodes. Since they were all in Bombay and the recording happened in Delhi, producers always looked for those from the film fraternity visiting Delhi to request to record an episode.

'I am proud to state that no one ever refused,' concludes Sharma. 'When the entire VBS setup moved to Bombay, things became simpler.'

We mention the remarks of Col Pande to our friends in Vividh Bharati and particularly highlight the fact that the programme aired simultaneously when the soldiers were free and relaxing.

'We planned it that way,' nods Mamta Singh in agreement. She is the better half of Yunus Khan. We had referred to them as the first couple of the Vividh Bharati service. Both are top-rated presenters on AIR and household names. They share a love for literature and were the only two selected through the same audition from thousands of applicants. She presents many programmes but is best known for *Sakhi Saheli*, a top-rated programme aimed at female listeners and a listeners' choice programme *Hello Saheli*.

Though some listeners' choice programmes have since been discontinued, *Sakhi Saheli* remains one of the most popular and has a consistent listenership, quite surprisingly it is also popular among men. It is broadcast from 3 p.m. to 4 p.m. Besides the film songs that are a staple of all Vividh Bharati programmes, *Sakhi Saheli* also has tips on health, information about the world and a consistent message about women's empowerment.

As an article in *The Indian Express* said in 2008:

> The announcers sound like friends engaged in a fun conversation—the language is kept simple, and the songs range from old melodies to new Hindi tunes. All are interspersed with candid, informative discussions. Sakhi Saheli, a synonym for girlfriend, is a popular show, undoubtedly.
>
> For a one-way medium, the show still manages a remarkable two-way conversation with listeners, from school students to senior citizens. They pen letters and postcards, sharing thoughts, short stories, poems and couplets; some write about the problems they encounter and overcome in their lives, including gender discrimination in their families. The radio hosts read these letters and start discussions on everything from good parenting to cultivating hobbies. As a result, Sakhi Saheli has a broad audience: rural, suburban and cosmopolitan listeners, including many men.

'Look at the brilliant positioning of the programme *Sakhi Saheli*,' says an ad executive, Rashmi Banerjee, who has been listening to it on and off for many years. 'The housewife has finished her chores and the children are back from school. She has served lunch and can now take a moment of respite. Then, her sahelis, friends from Vividh Bharati, engage with her, talking about recipes, home remedies and such, which are useful and entertaining. And between the talks are lovely songs.'

'The whole packaging is just perfect,' Rashmi concludes.

'Poet and former AIR Mumbai station director, Rajesh Reddy, conceived the programme,' says Mamta. 'He tried to ensure as much scope for interaction with audiences as possible. Beyond infotainment, the audience should be able to engage with the show personally. I think we achieved the objective and built on that.'

'It is about getting gyan in fun, while also getting entertained,' concludes Mamta.

We appreciate her videos on the Vividh Bharati Facebook page announcing a specific programme and seeking suggestions. We wonder if this is the new way of getting in touch with listeners and ask her that.

'Yes, of course,' she agrees and explains. 'Listeners' choice programmes continue in a different format today—they use social media.' Every programme is announced on Facebook and people comment on it. As a result, popular presenters like Mamta and Yunus receive around 1,000 daily comments that are pretty detailed and help them shape their programmes.

Taking of listener requests has largely been stopped, though there are programmes like *Hello Farmaish*; thus the listener's participation is by no means over. For example, in some programmes, the RJ announces the song and asks listeners to guess the movie, lead actor, lyricist or music director. Listeners have to send in a text message before the song is over. This is very popular and keeps listeners engaged. Still, alas, names like Jhumri Telaiya and Bhatapara no longer roll out of the radio sets into the consciousness of the listeners.

Old-timers lament the loss of the vast public connection generated by listeners' choice programmes. At the same time, the new generation argues that cost control and revenue generation are of prime importance these days and such indulgences are no longer affordable. We leave this issue for discussion with the top brass of Prasar Bharati.

The issue of revenue brings us back to why Vividh Bharati was conceptualized in the first place. One aspect was the loss of listeners to Radio Ceylon, but the connecting factor was revenue loss due to advertisers flocking to Radio Ceylon. So we take this up with a few old-timers.

In 1967, almost ten years after the start of broadcasts on Vividh Bharati, this factor was finally addressed. Experimental airing of spots and jingles started then. When Vividh Bharati celebrated its silver jubilee in 1982, around thirty-odd stations had begun to air advertisements and sponsored programmes.

Though not much information is available about the first spots or jingles aired on Vividh Bharati, Kamal Sharma tells us about some iconic sponsored programmes.

'The pharmaceutical company, Roche, was the first off the block in sponsoring a programme. On 3 May 1970, the first sponsored programme, *Saridon ke Saathi*, was aired at noon. Pushing its tablet Saridon, advertised as the instant cure for headaches, it had famous film stars talking about their co-stars. The first guest was Simi Garewal and the compere was the iconic Ameen Sayani of *Binaca Geetmala* fame. The programme's popularity can be gauged from the fact that the last episode of the series, featuring Kishore Kumar, was uploaded on YouTube in February 2021 and had already grossed three lakh views until October.'

'The same afternoon at 12.45 p.m. was the programme sponsored by Kohinoor Mills titled *Kohinoor Geet Gunjaar,*' continues Sharma. 'Another popular and long-running one was *Santogen ki Mehfil*, where comedians like Tun Tun and Mohan Choti enthralled the listeners. Old-time listeners remember programmes like *Cherry Blossom Nok Jhonk*, presented by Vijay Behl, Madhur Bhushan and her husband, Brij Bhushan. They also recall other sponsored programmes like one by Femina Textiles called *Johnny Walker ke Jawaah* and a programme from Khadi Gramodyog called *Azaadi ki Amar Kahani.*'

'During our schooldays, we listened to the *Bournvita Quiz Contest*. It was an eagerly awaited programme on AIR,' Sarita, a retired school teacher, recalls. 'For the first contest aired on 12 April 1972, auditions were conducted in schools and three teams were selected to participate in the radio show. So naturally, great prestige was attached to getting selected to participate in the contest and it attained cult status amongst schoolchildren. The participants were treated as the standard-bearers of the school's honour.'

Devangshu Datta, a consulting editor for the *Business Standard* newspaper, recalls how he and his teammates from St. Xavier's Collegiate School in Calcutta were regular participants in the show—they won the quiz thrice in a row from 1976 to 1978. 'We took up these internal tests (qualifiers) during free periods—we had a lot of free periods then,' Datta smiles as he says this. 'The most incredible excitement was travelling to Bombay and putting up in the Taj Mahal Hotel, besides seeing a live version of the famous radio programme in the (AIR) studio.'

The original quiz master on the radio show was Hamid Sayani, on whose death four years after the show started, his brother Ameen Sayani took over. It reached its zenith with a live show across cities with Derek O'Brien as the host and went on for a full twenty years before moving first to television, then in 2015 to YouTube and finally to an app. It was the precursor to most quiz shows and live quizzes in college fests. With this contest, Vividh Bharati had again created a genre where none existed in India and got a whole generation of schoolchildren addicted to the radio.

Another programme that received an immense fan following was *Inspector Eagle ke Kaarnamey*, featuring the lead character of the inspector and his entertaining sidekick, Havaldar Naik. Eagle Flasks sponsored the programme, hence the title Inspector Eagle. The idea for the popular television series *Karamchand* came from *Inspector Eagle*. It also inspired movies like *Do Jasoos*, which starred Raj Kapoor and Rajendra Kumar as the bumbling detectives. The radio show had a huge fan following and the new mystery revealed remained widely discussed the day after its transmission.

Many things have not changed on Vividh Bharati and quite a few formats have continued as initially conceived of many years ago, but it's not as if Vividh Bharati is frozen in time. Had that been so, its immense popularity, even to date, would have been impossible to sustain.

In the late '90s, for instance, branding changed. Rajesh Reddy, the then station director at Bombay, initiated the change. From *Panch Rangi Karyakram*, Vividh Bharati had the line '*Desh kee suurilee dhadhan*', which was more in tune with what was being broadcast. The earlier line was '*Akashvani kee manoranjan sewa*'.

Not only is the point of access for broadcasts changing from a fixed radio or a transistor set to a smartphone, but the nature of the programming is also slowly undergoing a significant localization. As a part of this drive, time slots are being provided to stations to create content in the local languages. In addition, the radio jockeys' speaking style has changed from a formal one to a more conversational one. Both these ensure a better and broader listener base and a better connect.

'Vividh Bharati connects across the country and across all age groups,' says Yunus Khan. 'Critics initially commented that being a

Hindi film song-based programme, we wouldn't find acceptability in the southern parts of India. Still, do you know where the maximum number of Mohammed Rafi fans are? Kerala! They even have a Mohammed Rafi Road in Kochi!' he concludes, his mop of curly hair bobbing with every movement of his head.

'Similarly, with many private radio stations now on the air, we are being told they have taken away our fifteen- to twenty-five-year-old listeners,' adds Jitendra. 'But do you think that's true? It just couldn't be. If that were true, no one in this age group would have heard of Mohammed Rafi or even Kishore Kumar! Hum a Kishore Kumar number in front of anyone in this age group—they will start humming it with you. If they haven't listened to Vividh Bharati—where have they heard the songs then?' The logic is unbeatable and the passion in their voices is palpable.

'Innumerable voices lie captured for posterity in the archives of Vividh Bharati, voices which have informed, enthralled, captivated and fascinated millions of people over the past many decades,' Patanjali Maduskar says, pride evident in his voice.

With a legacy like that and passion like this propelling it forward, we know Vividh Bharati will be the nation's heartbeat for many years.

Vividh Bharati is all about Indian film music, but there is a large body of music in India that is neither classical nor film music and yet captivates millions—the folk music genre.

We want to learn more about the support given to folk music by AIR and land at the doorstep of Sunaini Guleria Sharma in Chandigarh. She is an ethnomusicologist who is researching and resurrecting various forms of folk music from Punjab.

Her musical lineage is extremely illustrious as her maternal grandmother, Surinder Kaur, is a household name worldwide wherever Punjabi is spoken. Surinder Kaur's singing of folk music forms such as tappa, heer, mahia, dhola, suhaag, boliyaan, ghorian, etc., are the gold standards for their rendition.

Sunaini's mother, Dolly Guleria, took the baton forward and toured the world, bringing folk music from Sanjha Punjab (meaning the Punjabi-speaking areas in India and Pakistan) to Punjabi-speaking households.

We ask Sunaini about AIR's role in preserving these art forms.

'My grandmother picked up the songs from her mother, who sang them on festive occasions. However, had it not been for AIR, they would have remained within the kitchens and sung on ceremonial occasions for maybe one generation and would then have been lost. Since 1943, AIR provided the platform that enabled these to be recorded with accompaniment, preserved and played to millions of Punjabi-speaking people worldwide.' Sunaini tells us that she witnessed all this while staying with her grandparent sat school and college since her father, an army man, was posted across the nation.

'Grandma's whole life centred around radio and recordings,' she adds. 'She was either away recording or was busy with her accompanists and fellow performers preparing for the next ones. A successful recording always meant sweets for the kids and a party for the entire family.'

Sunaini tells us that not only did her grandmother and mother perform classical folk compositions but they also set the poetry of modern-day Punjabi poets of the likes of Shiv Batalvi, Prof. Mohan Singh, Prof. Harbhajan Singh, Nana Lal Noorpuri, Amrita Pritam, etc. These were all recorded and preserved by AIR. These poets became names in every Punjabi's mind only due to AIR's role in popularizing their poetry.

Sunaini mentions that it is due to the dignified patronage given by AIR that not only her grandmother and her grandaunt but many other women could come forward to perform, thus preserving an entire cultural tradition.

The phrase 'dignified patronage' used by Sunaini travels with us as we return to Delhi in the final lap of our journey, looking at the musical journey of AIR. We plan to look at another genre that would have succumbed years ago if it had not been for the role of AIR in its life cycle. The genre is Western classical music. We try to understand where Western music fits in.

9

Music: Western

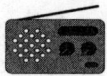

'WHEN MY FATHER WAS FRESH OUT OF THE INDIAN MILITARY Academy and was in his first posting, Colonel Wavell Smith was his commanding officer. Dad's seniors at the Academy had warned him that he was being posted to a unit where the CO was hard as nails and brooked no nonsense. Col Smith was reported to be a pure terror and just the idea of a summon to his office would send shivers down the toughest officer's spine. But come evening, he would be seen sitting on the porch of his bungalow, in his favourite rocking chair, a drink by his side, with Bach or Beethoven wafting through the air, a serene expression on his face.'

We are sitting with (retd) Brigadier O.P. Singh, a much-decorated veteran in his mid-eighties, reminiscing about his father, who rose to be a major general. Brig. Singh explains where he caught his love of Western classical music. 'Dad decided one day to listen to these himself to check out what it was that "tamed the beast" and got hooked himself, and since I grew up listening to this genre, I got hooked too!'

In the 1930s, the period that Brig. Singh speaks of, the broadcast of Western music was at its peak on AIR. A full three-fourths of all transmission time was then devoted to music, most of which was Western music. The reason was apparent—AIR was primarily created to entertain its colonial masters.

There was also a particular class of Indians, including royalty and the elite who wanted to ingratiate themselves with their colonial masters and heard Western music to imbibe the nuances and talk about them. Also, since Indian classical singers were initially reluctant to work on AIR, it was forced to draw their performers from amongst the dancing girls of Chawri Bazaar. They were considered women of 'easy virtue', and many listeners were reluctant to be seen as hearing music created by them and therefore switched to Western music. A huge listener base for Western classical music was thus created.

'This was when musicians like John Foulds, Walter Kauffman and Stephen Carrier, who worked for AIR, pushed for more broadcast times for Western classical music, which gained great acceptability,' says Patanjali Maduskar.

Khorshid Mancherji, a retired lawyer now settled in Mumbai, talks of when his family lived in Portuguese-occupied Silvassa, where they had huge landholdings.

'Those were the times when every well-to-do family in the Portuguese-occupied territories had a second home in Mumbai. We would often stay there for weeks and the main attraction of Mumbai for us was the clubbing. The singing, dancing and music were intrinsic to clubbing and we lived for that. The most popular sessions were when artistes invited from European clubs performed. AIR piggybacked on these clubs,' Khorshid tells us. 'They could not afford the artistes' fees, so they broadcast live performances from the clubs. The clubs permitted them to do this free of charge since AIR announced the names of the clubs during the programmes and they got free publicity. It was a win-win for both and Western music won many a follower in the process.'

When even this form of programming was not available, there were always the army and police bands and when they were too busy, choir music from churches was broadcast. Though most bands had heavy orchestration and could hardly play anything besides martial music, some, like the Viceroy's Orchestra and the Royal Air Force band, played classical pieces.

'The '40s were when all forms of Western music were available to the listeners,' says Brig. Singh. 'So AIR played symphonies, sonatas, etc., and relayed club and pop from the clubs while army bands contributed the martial music. As all choir music is based on Western classical music, its broadcast also helped popularize the genre,' he explains.

'A devoted listenership developed for jazz too and all the kids in our family learnt to play some instrument. I blow a mean trumpet even at this age,' boasts Khorshid.

'It was also a question of the one who paid the piper calling the tune,' says Derek Symonds, senior announcer in the Western classical music section in AIR Delhi since 2003. 'A license was required to own a radio then and the funds collected went to AIR. The licenses continued to be needed till the '60s almost. A survey of license holders in 1936 showed that nearly 50 per cent in Delhi, over 55 per cent in Calcutta and 44 per cent in Bombay wanted to listen to European music. Since this far exceeded the number of British license holders, it was clear that many Indians were listening to European music. So European music in all its forms got firmly ensconced in AIR.'

Tony Pinto, a retired music teacher in Calcutta who used to play the piano in five-star hotels for many years, says, 'During the '40s, many experimentations went into Western music broadcasts. Walter Kauffman, for instance, created the opera *Anasuya*. Similarly, Liza Lehmann set the *Rubaiyat of Omar Khayyam* to classical music. These experiments were designed to make inroads for Western music in the minds of the Indian listeners and succeeded very well in the effort. Typically, Western instruments like violin, cello and clarinet were introduced to the listeners in this country and went on to be adopted into the Indian musical systems. That we have pure Indian classical ragas played not only on the violin, but even on the guitar and instruments such as the mandolin is a tribute to the work put in then.'

Pinto tells us that Kauffman initially found Indian music 'alien and incomprehensible'. He is, however, quoted as saying, 'As I knew that people with heart and intellect created this music, one could assume that many, in fact, millions would be appreciating or loving this music and I concluded that the fault was all mine. The right way would be to undertake a study tour to the place of its origin.' He explored the genre extensively and the results are for all to see.

Incidentally, the signature tune of AIR was also composed by Kauffman in the raga Shivaranjani and AIR continues to use it even today. The violinist, Mehli Mehta, the father of Zubin Mehta, the famous conductor, is credited with playing the tune.

The Second World War dampened the festivities but introduced a format into radio listening. A new programme called *You Asked for It* was introduced, based on the need of the Allied soldiers posted in India to stay connected to their families and their sweethearts. It broadcast the families' messages and played their requests and was a precursor to all the listeners' choice programmes broadcast to date, and was so popular that it got up to 500 letters a week.

The star who compiled and compered this programme lit up the firmament of Indian broadcasting for years and years after that—it was none other than Melville de Mellow!

'Melville meticulously read all the letters, wrote down the messages and created a script around them,' gushes veteran broadcaster Basudha Banerji, whom we met earlier. She is a die-hard Melville fan and informs us that the show lasted a full thirty-five weeks.

'The shows that followed introduced many names to Indian broadcasting. Names like Kenneth Parker, V.M. Chakrapani, Quinee Sundaram, Deepa Jai Singh, Hilda Flanders and Melville carried the torch of Western music well into the '60s,' Basudha informs us.

AIR had, by then, acquired a very respectable collection of Western music, which led Richard Blanchette, a journalist from the BBC, to remark once that the Western music collection of AIR was amongst the best in the world.

'When I was first posted to the Western music section in the late '80s and early '90s, I thought I was in for a relaxing time since I had a working knowledge of Western classical music and a decent enough liking for it. However, when I first stepped into the studios, boy, was I intimidated,' says Manoj, the veteran broadcaster we had met while talking of the magazine section for the features unit.

'All the announcers I heard compering these programmes then were either ex-IAS or even ex-ICS officers, ex-ambassadors, professors, etc. They came in dressed in three-piece suits, neckties knotted just right, matching kerchiefs stylishly jutting out of their pockets and puffing at their cigars or cheroots before entering the studios. Even the chair they sat on in the Western music studio was like a throne, ornately carved with brass inlay work done on it.'

'The contact with these stars made me who I am today,' confesses Manoj. 'They worked on my diction and pronunciation. For example, they made me say "Bey-tho-vuhn" and "Moht-zart" until I got every word right and it started a lifelong love affair with diction and the obsession with pronouncing every word correctly.'

During a 'World Radio Day' organized by the United Nations in Delhi, many presenters confessed they had learned the correct way of speaking English from Manoj. Quite a few even came and touched his feet as a gesture of respect, something for which Manoj thanks his stint in the Western music section.

'I remember listening to a lot of Western music on the radio until the mid-'90s,' says Meera Johri, a sixty-year-old publishing house owner. 'Mornings particularly were set aside for Western music as I rushed through the daily chores, getting the children ready and preparing to go to the office. Mornings from 8 to 9 were always for pop music for me and Rihanna and Beyonce wafted through my house. The one-hour slot from 9 a.m. onwards was for the *Matchless Music Hour*, which mainly played retro hits. However, I lost track of time after that as work was very demanding. Before I slept, though, I made it a point to listen to soothing classical music or jazz.'

'This was the golden age of Western music on AIR,' agrees Manoj. 'CEOs of companies and embassy staffers heard the broadcasts. Some of the comments we got were in such great detail that it was an education for us.'

Unfortunately, a minor disaster struck Western music on AIR Delhi station in the early 1980s. A survey for the audience research unit conducted by a private agency revealed that most Western music programmes had less than 1.1 per cent listenership. Some, like *Clarion Call*, *Wicked Hours* and *Words and Music*, had zero listenership and these were naturally axed, reducing the time allotted to Western music. This led to massive outrage and many, like the noted lawyer Soli Sorabjee, fumed against the move.

'This is a very wrong and retrograde move. Western music is Western only in name but is universal in appeal. It is very much liked and enjoyed by the people,' he complained.

His ire was understandable since he was a jazz enthusiast and a passionate trumpet player. The programme *All the Jazz* had also been reported as having zero listenership and had been discontinued.

However, broadcasts on Calcutta, Mumbai, Goa and all Northeast stations continued. 'The Northeast has many talented composers and bands and a lot of programming comes through for these stations,' confirms Andrews. 'The best of the lot is from Mizoram and Nagaland and the orchestra there is also relatively strong and performs regularly, which is why they were not touched.'

Many Western music lovers floated a conspiracy theory about how someone deliberately misled the research team, whereas others complained about the sample's representativeness. The damage, however, was done.

The introduction of the FM channels in the late '90s—Vividh Bharati for Hindi film music, 'Gold' for infotainment and 'Rainbow' for classy entertainment—formed the triumvirate that ruled the airwaves for AIR. FM Rainbow consisted of a series of local channels broadcast from all the main stations branded as one, enabling content localization. Delhi, Mumbai, Goa, Guwahati, Kolkata and a host of stations in the Northeast all had their Western music broadcasts aired on this channel. The advantage of the FM Rainbow channel was crystal clear reception. The channel in Delhi broadcast Hindi and English music in the proportion of one hour of English for every three hours of Hindi broadcasts.

FM Rainbow Delhi had six hours of Western music, while Kolkata, Mumbai and Goa had about eight hours each. The Northeast, of course, had more than eight hours per day.

Private channels had just appeared and amongst the first were 'Times FM' (now called Radio Mirchi) and 'Radio One'. All the private FM channels' content was also uplinked from the AIR facilities. As per the terms of their contract, they got nine hours of peak timing in the day, leaving AIR with fifteen hours, nine of which were at night.

On its face, it seemed as if AIR did not have the peak hours for itself and would get only residual listenership, but the reverse happened. A classic example was a programme called *Wicked Hour*, which was discontinued as per the earlier survey but brought back to fill the post-midnight slot.

'This was an announcer's choice programme aired from 1 a.m. to 2 a.m. The announcer played tracks as per his choice, primarily soft and soulful ones, keeping the time slot in mind. So we could play what we wanted except party music, which was inappropriate for the time slot. Besides, a programme called *Footloose* broadcast daily between 9 p.m. to 10 p.m. also featured this genre,' confirms Sunil Gupta.

The rule at that time, strictly enforced by Ms Linda, who headed the Western music unit, was that every rookie would first get this slot. This is where Raman Bhanot, then a fresher straight out of college with just a year or two of Yuvavani experience behind him, landed. In just one single night, while presenting it, Raman, now a leading sportscaster, discovered the power of radio.

'"What have you done on the *Wicked Hour* on your first night out?" Seema, who managed the tape library, asked me when I walked over to her to collect my tapes for the night's programme,' reminisces Raman. 'I didn't know how to react, wondering whether I had committed a blunder. "Have you seen the mail that has come in?" she asked me. I accessed the mail and reading it, sat down with a thump, overcome with emotion,' says he.

That day, he had played a number by Mr Big, titled 'Goin' Where the Wind Blows', and also spoken a few words about life having a direction of its own and about how we need to surrender to the flow and let nature run its course.

'The mail was from Ashok Bhatnagar, who heard the programme with his terminally ill brother as he sat by his side keeping the night-time vigil. Hearing the song, my commentary and the other songs of the night, which were on similar themes, both brothers had connected, cried and finally found peace and acceptance.' Raman's voice still slurs with the emotional impact of recounting it and we have goosebumps.

Another show that Raman hosted with much success was a request-based show called *Live Wire*, hosted by luminaries such as Roshan Abbas and well-known RJs, Yuri and Param, before him. He went on to host it for almost five years. It was such a hit that listeners practically identified the show with him.

'It was a request show,' he recounts. 'People wrote letters and emails and sent messages requesting I play certain songs for the "someone special" in their lives. The programme's prime attraction was that it was a live "dial-in-dial-out" show.'

This meant that he had two telephone lines in front of him in the studios and as soon as he played a number, he took calls on them. He screened the calls, put them on hold and took them live, as soon as the number finished playing.

'This was a major challenge since I had to manage the tapes playing the numbers simultaneously with the ones playing the advertising clips and make outcalls.'

He explains that many shy of coming live online would leave phone numbers asking him to call back in a 'dial out'. He would do so and then speak out the messages on the caller's behalf.

'What if they were too mushy?' we ask him.

'I would then modify them and say the same thing in my own words,' he says, smiling at the memories.

'And didn't the men think that you, with your tall, dark and handsome looks (he had already started doing television by then) and seductive voice, would run away with their girls?' we ask him.

'I guess they realized they could trust me,' he laughs as he says this and we guffaw and take leave.

They say that all good things come to an end, as did this run on FM Rainbow Delhi. On 16 August 2021, another order was received by which Western music was shifted from FM Rainbow to FM Gold. The hours were cut from seven to five and many popular programmes were axed.

Suddenly, listeners from Delhi were deprived of their favourite fix since FM Gold was not quite as popular. A recently retired producer confirmed that the station was inundated with emails asking why the change was made. Listeners again deserted the Delhi station and started looking for alternatives.

The silver lining is that the FM Rainbow stations countrywide are now accessible at the flick of a finger on the NewsOnAir app. As a result, many from Delhi listen to Rita Dias from Mumbai, Sachin Chatte from Goa and a host of talented casual announcers from these stations and those from the Northeast. So, what Delhi has lost is made up elsewhere.

We ask Derek Symonds about jazz and he confirms that it is back on Wednesday and Friday nights on FM Gold.

We talk to many lay listeners, some of whom may not be regular listeners of Western music programmes and all agree that this should not be permitted to die down as a genre. Just as film music and light music forms like ghazals, bhajans, etc., would be poorer if Indian classical music were ignored, so would many light music compositions, including film music be if Western music were sidelined. Many light music compositions use instruments like the piano, the saxophone, or the trumpet, to learn, for which a solid grounding in Western classical music is essential.

Think back to old Hindi movies where the spurned hero would sit down on the piano, an essential accessory in the villain's drawing room, and sing his broken heart melodies. Would they be the same on any other instrument?

'We have a fantastic collection of recordings in our archives, though they need to be taken care of. Many pieces are available with us that are probably not there with anyone in Asia. They can and are being shared nationwide and regularly heard,' concludes Derek.

Manoj has the last word. 'We have the most extensive collection of jazz instruments in the world. Every city, town and village grooves to the tunes played on them at least for a few months every year.' He hums a few songs and as our feet tap to them instinctively, we understand he is talking about the brass bands without which no Indian wedding is complete. We think back to the tunes they play and to which we dance at weddings and realize most of them are based on Western music compositions. We smile and are hopeful.

10

The Future

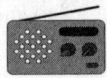

'THERE IS NO FUTURE FOR AIR' IS A COMMON REFRAIN THAT worries us. Yet, in crafting this book, we have met countless broadcasters, media watchers and lay listeners and have been deeply impressed by the dedication of AIR's staffers. We have felt the deep love of its listeners for the medium and have been overawed by its sterling legacy. The remotest possibility that it may not survive or was on a self-destruct mission disturbs us deeply. However, many have told us this, particularly the ex-staffers who have gone on and on about the golden days before 'revenue generation' and 'cost-cutting' became buzzwords.

With this in mind, we decide to chat with Shashi Shekhar Vempati, who joined the board of Prasar Bharati in February 2016 and was the CEO from June 2017 to June 2022, to understand the sweeping changes that took place during his tenure.

Vempati is a distinguished-looking IIT graduate who has spent much of his career with Infosys, the information technology major. He was the first non-broadcaster, non-bureaucrat to head the organization and has often been pilloried for not knowing broadcasting, being uncaring about the needs of the staff and being excessively focused on cost-cutting to the detriment of quality.

When we spoke to some of the staffers, some even accused him of being the agent of the powers that be who was assigned the job of closing down AIR, so that the prime land on which AIR stations sit could be sold to private developers.

We are surprised to find a pleasant, smiling gentleman, unlike the stern-faced, serious-looking ex-CEO we expected to meet and we begin by asking him about the 'great sell-off'.

'Did they not mention that the deal has already been negotiated and buyers identified?' He guffaws and adds that many also accused him of being the agent of a few top industrial houses.

'Is AIR on the verge of shutting down any time in the future?' We come to the point straight away, and he responds thoughtfully.

'I can assure you that AIR is here to stay. It is not going anywhere. What will change is that it will become a trimmer, nimbler organization that will meet the challenges of the current market scenario. Also, the way people access radio is changing significantly. Digital is the way forward and that is where the future lies. Yes, I agree that there is a great deal of doubt and uncertainty in employees' minds, causing frustration, but that is inevitable when there is a major change. I took many steps during my tenure to cut the slack, rationalize operations, eliminate the patronage and entitlement economy and go digital. These may slow down with the new regime, which consists of bureaucrats whose priorities and way of operation may differ from mine, but the trajectory once set cannot change,' he asserts.

During his tenure as the CEO of Prasar Bharati, Vempati pioneered many initiatives to rationalize analogue terrestrial networks. He oversaw the expansion of AIR's FM network while accelerating its digital presence through new-age platforms like Amazon Alexa. His vision was to modernize AIR (and Doordarshan) to adapt to the new reality of content primarily accessed through digital devices. The emphasis was on making radio available on mobile phones, uploading content on YouTube channels, increasing interaction with listeners and promoting content via social media handles to increase engagement.

Under his leadership, Digital Prasar Bharati encompassed 350+ active social media handles, the same number of active YouTube channels and twenty-plus live streams. In December 2022, the AIR mobile application delivered content to over twenty million listeners, growing by a healthy two million every month since September 2022. In addition, both AIR and Doordarshan reach forty million-plus households through its free-to-air DTH platform—DD Free Dish.

However, an emphasis on cost-cutting, revenue generation and rationalization of staff structure characterized Vempati's tenure. During our interaction with many staffers and ex-staffers, we have heard about curbs on expenses, phasing out some programmes that did not have the potential to generate revenue and the massive reduction in staff strength. They roundly criticized him for hampering creativity, curtailing artistic freedom and changing the role of the public service broadcaster to that of a purely commercial one. The commonly held opinion was that his actions sidelined the country's cultural legacy. We want to know this first, so we ask him about the 'harsh steps' he took as CEO.

Vempati explains, 'As per Prasar Bharati Act, the Government of India transferred all the assets of AIR and Doordarshan to this corporation in 1997, but it is not a corporation in the true sense; it is a statutory autonomous body. So, many sanctions still come from the ministry, but the funds don't.'

We had presumed the Prasar Bharati Act allows for government support, but he tells us the government did not fund even the budgetary deficit. So we ask him how much this is and he flips through a set of papers and tells us that in 2022–23, the expenses projection was over ₹700 crore, and the revenue was ₹300 crore.

The entire deficit, Vempati informs us, is met by internal revenue generation. In the current scenario, it is from the surplus funds of Doordarshan.

'This is not a solution feasible in the long run. So, quite naturally, fiscal prudence was a necessity. All I tried was to cut the slack and reduce the inefficiencies. What options do we have?' He throws up his hand and bends forward to emphasize the point. His tone acquires an intensity we had not noticed before: 'We understand that such shakeups are never easy, but like surgery—if you want to recover, you must go through it.'

Vempati explains further, 'As per the Act, employees recruited for AIR and Doordarshan before 5 October 2007 continue to remain government employees and those recruited later are employees of Prasar Bharati. The Government of India pays only the wages, pensions and related expenses of the first category of employees. So all the operational expenses, including the salaries of the post-2007 recruited employees, have to be funded by revenue generation from commercial advertising and sponsorship and whatever other commercial activities Prasar Bharati can undertake. This is a massive challenge because nowhere does a public broadcaster sustain itself through advertising. In India, we did it because of the unique model where operations must be funded from our revenues.'

He cites the example of the BBC, often used as a benchmark for comparisons during our conversations about the state of AIR.

'Do you know that the BBC gets a proportion of the license fee levied for radio sets, almost ₹33,000 crores in Indian currency equivalent? This is when their network is not even a tenth of ours. So where is the comparison?' he asks rhetorically.

We recollect being told by one of his aides about the drive to make the office operations efficient, faster and paperless. He informs us that this has been implemented in all the 577 offices of Prasar Bharati by mid-2021.

'The average time for clearing a file has gone down from seven days to twenty-four hours,' Vempati tells us. 'Not only has the efficiency increased, but the system's manipulation by some unscrupulous employees has also been eliminated,' he adds.

Cost-cutting has also meant closing down all the analogue transmitters and phasing out shortwave transmission. Most listeners are tuned to medium wave transmissions with a smaller range but better quality or to FM transmissions. Replacing shortwave transmitters with digital ones made sense. In addition, Prasar Bharati closed all terrestrial transmission towers since transmission is satellite-based now.

'Engineers were switching on towers sitting in the offices and then switching them off and going home. Where was the economic sense in that?' he asks us. He adds that some towers were converted into FM relay stations, which has increased listenership.

'Not a single radio station closed down, nor has any been converted into a relay station, nor is any closure proposed,' Vempati is emphatic when we ask him. 'Yes, programming is rationalized, but that is necessary to survive.'

He explains that there was a rationalization of programmes underway. He gives us the example of Delhi, where two FM channels, Rainbow and Gold, broadcast film music, often simultaneously. This meant that the same listeners were divided into two channels and two sets of people were employed to cater to them.

'We decided to do away with the duplication and as a result, naturally, some staffers became redundant. How many radio jockeys do you think an FM channel has on average?' he stops the narrative and asks us. We guess it is probably three or four, to which he agrees with a nod before delivering the statistic about overstaffing that shocks us.

'And can you guess how many became redundant due to this exercise at FM Gold alone? Eighty. Eighty were employed when only four or five would have sufficed. Of course, they were not full-time employees but were called on a contract basis, but think of how much overstaffing just one channel had. When we explored this for other stations, we found up to five verticals in some cases and five sets of people were called up on a contractual basis to handle them. This was a major racket and a colossal patronage economy existed. We made everything online and such selections transparent, naturally creating outrage among the beneficiaries. Most of the noise came from them and since many are politically influential, it got amplified.' Vempati shrugs as if to state that this is a part of working for the government.

Vibhav Behl, a young journalist covering media for a prominent newspaper chain, talks about this.

'After the "sacking" of the DJs, there was a big agitation. It was made out as if eighty people had been deprived of their livelihood. No one clarified that this livelihood was not theirs in the first place because they were all part-timers, otherwise gainfully employed elsewhere, who only used this either for pocket money or to create personal brands. They collaborated with some vested interests, took the matter to Parliament, misguided a few hon'ble MPs and got them to ask the minister questions. However, when the facts came out, matters settled down.'

Behl informs us that there was a big racket at some levels and many unscrupulous staffers were calling up their favourites for the broadcasts. There were times when three or four outsiders were called to the studios and paid for one or two-minute sound bites within a fifteen-minute broadcast. This was justified on the 'creative requirement' plea but resulted in a massive expenditure. Staffers subsequently took the calling of contract staff as a right and entitlement and a patronage economy of enormous proportions flourished. Therefore, there was massive discontent when the reduction of duplication and the efficiencies of the paperless office concept curtailed this.

Behl tells us that by one estimate, as many as 5,000 employees were surplus in AIR. We recollect a music producer of AIR telling us that eight staffers were previously handling the portfolio he was now managing alone. It seems logical that the section was overstaffed; otherwise, the quality of the programmes would have deteriorated with the reduction in staff strength.

We talk to Vishvas Naniwadekar, a one-time contractual newsreader-cum-translator in the Marathi news unit of AIR. The conversation with him seems to confirm this fact of overstaffing, too.

'When I was on the panel, fifteen others were with me, with only three permanent employees. There were three news bulletins in a day and the permanent staffers arranged the roster so that one permanent newscaster and two part-timers would be on duty together. We part-timers would report on time and do most of the translation work, whereas they would come in an hour before the bulletin time, check our work and read the news.'

We learn from him that in some instances, the full-time staff members worked only three and a half days a week with a two-hour presence constituting a workday.

This massive overstaffing, which led to financial unviability, was noticed early on. A special committee led by Sam Pitroda was set up in 2014 to review the work of Prasar Bharati and one of its significant recommendations was to conduct a workforce audit. The I&B ministry assigned this job to the department of expenditure, which dragged its feet on the matter for four years. Finally, in 2018, E&Y was awarded the job. Their report indicated that staff salaries accounted for 60 per cent of Prasar Bharati's expenses compared to 30 per cent for BBC.

We ask Vempati how he tried to reduce the workforce in a governmental set-up where retrenchment was not an option. He tells us that staff strength could be brought down only by rationalizing portfolios as people retire.

'We have also started replacing the retiring employees with contractual ones. As a result, there will be cost-cutting, but there will also be a churning of ideas every time a new person takes over,' is his response.

Vempati does not say and we infer, that with most of the employees being contractual, the sense of entitlement amongst staffers would also be eliminated. Also, the organization would become nimbler, with reassignment and replacement becoming real-time options when efficiencies were compromised.

A casual glance at the vacancies page on the Prasar Bharati website confirms this trend. All the scheduled recruitments on the page are either contractual or, in a few cases, on deputation from other government departments. The salary offered to news editor-cum-presenter on the page in January 2022 is between ₹70,000 to ₹80,000, probably half of what a full-timer gets currently. We ask Vempati whether this emolument level would get the necessary talent into AIR. He emphatically replies in the affirmative, citing the examples of Rajya Sabha TV, a channel he ran from August 2017 to May 2019.

'I ran the channel with just three full-time staffers, with all the others being contractual. It saw phenomenal growth during this period and the YouTube channel added two million subscribers. So if it worked there, it will work here too.'

Another finding of the E&Y survey stands out like a sore thumb—the engineers versus programming staff ratios. The study, completed in February 2021, reveals that 50 per cent of the staff of Prasar Bharati was engineering staff and only 20 per cent handled programming compared to 10 per cent and 70 per cent for the BBC. This clearly indicates a massive overstaffing in the engineering function. Of course, the BBC runs ten national and forty local radio stations, whereas AIR runs over 400, accounting for which, too, is a gross imbalance.

While talking to AIR staffers, we noticed a lot of discontent on this issue, mainly because many engineers got promoted faster.

'An engineer who was my engineering assistant when I was a transmission executive is now the station director whereas I have only moved up one notch to be programme executive,' a prominent musician working for AIR had complained.

Another one had also pointed out that as the engineers in top positions had no cultural background, they often created situations that would be laughable if not tragic. A classic example was when a producer went to his immediate boss for approval for a programme on the noted classical musician Pandit Bhimsen Joshi in his centenary year. The programme was sanctioned, but at the end of the meeting, the station director, an engineer, turned to the musician and asked, 'Who is this Joshi whose centenary you want to celebrate?' No doubt the engineer had no clue about the status of the Bharat Ratna awardee!

Listening to this anecdote, we could well imagine the frustration levels in the minds of the creative people forced to report to people without knowledge of their domain.

We attempt to trace the origins of this imbalance and turn to Behl again.

'Part of this is because of the phasing out of obsolete technologies,' he explains. 'The technologies went, but the staff, being government servants, could not be phased out as service rules protected them. So they came to occupy the only available positions—the administrative and managerial ones.'

He tells us that the only solution for rectifying the imbalance lies in time, as many will retire over the years and could be replaced with staffers in the programming cadre. Still, this explanation does not clarify why the programming staff got only one promotion against the three or four for the engineering staff.

V.K. Mohan, a Supreme Court lawyer handling many cases related to the media, explains this.

'The programming staff were divided into many categories: the transmission executives, the programme executives, the India Information service officers, the Central Secretariat service officers, those on contract and others on deputation. The engineering and programming cadres were both strongly unionized, but the engineering staff were more united. In contrast, the programming staff had an assortment of unions, with unions even existing in each branch of the service for different regions and castes. They were continuously litigating against each other on parity issues in rank, privileges and salary levels. So, they languished where they were,' Mohan concludes.

Vempati throws up his hands in despair when we ask him about the lack of promotions to programme staffers.

'My heart bleeds for them,' he says. 'It is a tragedy that people languish just one level above where they were recruited and retired as executives, but what can I do? My office handled over a thousand legal cases, hardly 10 per cent related to commercial disputes—the rest were all staff-related cases. There are hundreds of judgements on record, each prohibiting one or another action taken to sort out this problem. I could not promote, recruit or get people on deputation to many posts. The net result is that Prasar Bharati was forced to accept people from other services and cadres, leading to further charges of insensitivity.'

We sit with Prakash Javadekar, ex-minister of information and broadcasting and a member of the Rajya Sabha. He is a soft-spoken individual, dapper in appearance, who shows no signs of tiredness despite returning just minutes earlier from a gruelling eight-hour session in Parliament. He talks to us passionately for an hour about the future of AIR, against the ten minutes he had initially allotted us.

'The problem is serious,' he agrees with us. 'Accepting the reality that we could not reduce the strength of the engineering staff except by retirement, I proposed that each radio station have a creative head drawn from amongst the programming staff with appropriate levels between the production executive level and the creative head. All the programming staff would report only to the creative head, who would be one of them, and the engineers could be adjusted in all the other functions such as marketing, administration, etc., but it got stuck in red tape and never materialized,' he sighs.

He offers us a special 'Javadekar' sandwich, consisting of some delicious Marathi red chutney and butter spread over toasted slices of bread. The conversation drifts to his family, interests and the city of Pune. It is raining outside and he graciously offers us umbrellas and deputes someone to walk us to our car. We leave with the pleasant feeling of having met a complete gentleman.

Vempati acknowledges the contribution of Javadekar in unravelling this Gordian knot and accepts that this is probably the best proposal that could be formulated for sorting this out.

'I was able to get this through the ministry and we also made some appointments on a contractual basis. They were beginning to do good work, but after I left, some vested interests got together and in typical bureaucratic ways, hounded these appointees till they left. There are some immensely talented and dedicated people in that cadre and I respect their contribution to making AIR what it is, and I did my best to help them get their due. In the government, though, change can only be slow and often moves in fits and starts—I tried and maybe at some time in the future,' Vempati lets the sentence hang and the disappointment shows clearly on his face.

We are reminded of the statement of Nirmal Chatterjee, ex-director of the News Services Division. In his book

Mass Communication published in 1973, he wrote, 'AIR's staffers have chronic discontent about their status and employment prospects, an almost openly critical attitude to AIR's policy and programme and yet a remarkable loyalty to the institution in performing their duties.'

We agree completely.

We now turn to the most significant external threat to AIR—the private stations broadcasting on the FM channels.

Casual conversations with people in AIR tell us that while most people listen to private channels for a while, they ultimately return to Vividh Bharati. However, this seems slightly shaky when we talk to people on the road and ask them what radio stations they listen to. Most come back with names like Red FM, Radio Mirchi, Radio City, MY FM, etc.—all private channels. We also note that RJs on private channels have cult status on social media and are local celebrities, which means many people listen to them. We realize that even the term RJ was popularized only by the private channels.

An example is RJ Kartik of 94.3 MY FM, who is so immensely connected on social media that his Facebook page has sixty-four lakh likes. The figure is astonishing as he works at the Jaipur station of 94.3 MY FM, which can only be heard within the Jaipur district, which in December 2020 had an estimated population of just seventy-four lakh. His fan following very clearly is from all over the country. We commonly see the FM or frequency modulation technology as the one on which most channels broadcast and we want to find out what makes it so popular.

We ask Sumit Mohapatra, a telecom engineer with a private channel, who explains, 'The technology first came to the USA early this century. It enabled the broadcast of superb stereophonic sound over much shorter distances than the conventional AM broadcasts. In India, FM broadcasting began on an experimental basis in 1977, and up to 1993, AIR continued to be the only broadcaster in the game. Broadcasts in those days consisted of songs playing continuously without anyone speaking in between. In 1993, AIR gave some slots to private operators. The Times of India group, amongst others, gained considerable traction with its channel, Times FM. All these were stopped in 1998 when the government decided to auction the frequencies. In the year 2000, the government auctioned 108 frequencies nationwide and opened the floodgates.'

Behl adds, 'Today, AIR has 450 FM stations covering 39 per cent of the country's area and 52 per cent of the population. Against this, over 500 private radio stations broadcast to the same audience and have edged AIR for the top ranking in many markets.'

We now want to probe this external threat and meet Rahul J. Namjoshi, the CEO of 94.3 MYFM, a channel run by the DB group which also publishes the *Dainik Bhaskar*, an extremely popular Hindi newspaper. The channel 94.3 MYFM, present as a matter of strategy in tier two and tier three cities only, operates thirty radio stations and is a market leader in many of them. It is one of the biggies, along with Radio Mirchi, Radio City, Big FM and Orange. Besides these, many local and regional players also populate the FM broadcast space.

We ask Rahul what drives private radio stations and keeps them afloat in the highly competitive market.

'Our target market is the eighteen- to thirty-five-year-old group in tier two and three markets. It is not only the largest demographic group, but also the highest spending one and hence our entire effort is on engaging with them at all levels,' he responds. 'This means playing the kind of music they want to hear, speaking their language, making the broadcasts high on energy, offering relevant information and conducting offline events.'

We connect with Kartik Sharma, or RJ Kartik, as he is popularly known, to see what makes him such a sensation.

He is a smart-looking, bearded young man who, when accompanying his uncle to the local radio station at eighteen, got an opportunity to get behind the microphone for the first time—and has stayed hooked since. He has spent eleven years behind the microphone, most at 94.3 MY FM and has seen the evolution of FM broadcasting from close quarters.

'It is crucial to keep the customer engaged with the channel at all times,' he says. 'This does not only mean playing the kind of music they want but also designing the shows around their needs and giving them information relevant to their current needs. So, for example, we have an early morning show where we talk about astrological predictions and the religious significance of the day, an afternoon programme talking about women-centric themes and specific time slots for the school and college-going listeners. Outside experts add value to the broadcast by giving relevant information.'

We tell Rahul that there are similar shows on AIR and ask him how the FM channels differ. He informs us that the difference lies in the songs the RJs on FM channels play and their language while communicating with their listeners.

'All private FM channels work on the CHR (contemporary hit radio) format and hence only play current popular music, a bulk of which is Bollywood or Hindi film music. Also, the RJs speak the language of the young listeners, which is informal and high on energy,' Rahul explains.

'I do the breakfast show,' says RJ Kartik, 'and it is often quite chilly when I leave my house. Just yesterday, when I wanted to say I had skipped my bath, I said it was so cold that I had bathed with my deo (deodorant). The wisecrack went down very well with my listeners and I got numerous messages on social media later saying they loved the expression deo-bath.'

Rahul tells us that all the shows are always compered live to keep the energy and enthusiasm high and RJs also take feedback on social media into account while tailoring the spiel, unlike AIR, where many programmes are now prerecorded from the archives.

'We are nimbler and more energetic,' concludes Rahul, 'hence we keep the listener more engaged.'

This makes sense to us and we ask him about the outside events they conduct, which is, again, something AIR does not do.

He tells us about events in shopping malls and other public places where all kinds of zany contests take place and gifts, such as motorcycles, mobile phones, etc., are given to winners. He tells us about the *Paison ka Ped* event conducted in peak season in shopping malls nationwide.

'We create an artificial tree in the middle of the mall and dangle ropes from it. We ask contestants to hold on to the rope and stand under the tree. The one whose hand leaves the rope even for a moment gets eliminated and the last man standing wins ₹3 lakh. People queue up to participate and winners have stood for up to seventy-five hours!' he informs us with a twinkle in his eye, seeing our surprised looks.

Kartik talks about the Jal Mahal in Jaipur, visited by tourists from all over the world, whose surroundings had become filthy. 'We ran a campaign in collaboration with the municipal corporation of Jaipur to clean the city and saw people from the mayor onwards lining up to offer free time to the campaign. So not only did the place get cleaned up, but we also got attention as a socially responsible channel,' he proudly concludes. 'Such events are win-win for everyone and cost the channel nothing since advertisers sponsor the prizes. It gets them visibility and 94.3 MY FM receives engagement.'

'Twenty-five per cent of the revenue of 94.3 MY FM now comes from offline events,' states Rahul.

With the difference in the content and presentation and different methods of understanding listeners, we now turn to profitability and ask Rahul about its centrality to his operations.

He answers by saying that the core focus was always on profitability and the internal rate of return ruled all expenses.

The teams are given stiff sales targets, which are monitored and followed up relentlessly.

'Bosses are responsible for the performance of their teams and if the team underperforms, even the boss loses his incentive,' says Rahul.

We ask Neha Vadehra Arora, head of human resources at 94.3 MY FM, about the staff strength. The youngish-looking HR head astounds us by telling us that they generate a revenue of almost ₹150 crore with a staff strength of just a little over 500.

'Of these, almost half are sales staff, about 150 are programming staff and the rest are either engineers or administrative and support staff,' she adds in response to our query.

We casually ask about the number of engineers and almost do a backflip when informed that they employ only fifty to sixty engineers for all this. Even accounting for the fact that AIR runs fourteen times as many radio stations and operates across the country in more than one format, the count of engineers in AIR at 10,000-plus seems gargantuan. So, the point about downsizing the staff strength made by Vempati appears to make much more sense.

Rahul tells us that in fortnightly meetings, he personally monitors all costs.

'Even if a station buys a mop against the set norms, it is brought to my notice,' he emphatically states. 'Each increase in overheads, including additional recruitments, must be cleared by me. I am a bit lenient while sanctioning staff strength in sales since they generate revenue, but ask for an extra admin staffer and I will debate the proposal for hours before sanctioning it.'

We are reminded of the eighty-two RJs on AIR's Rainbow FM channel and we ask Rahul how many RJs each of his stations have. He says that each station has between four and five and stuns us by adding that they sometimes operate two radio stations each.

'Let me give an example: we broadcast from Nasik and Dhule in Maharashtra,' he explains. 'However, we do not have a studio in Dhule since the revenue does not justify the expense; we only have a tower. So, we create the content in the Nasik studios and broadcast it from the Dhule tower. So the same RJ could be live in Nasik for an hour and then go live in Dhule. For this, not only does the RJ change his accent and the nature of the local content, but we also change the studio lighting and a lit-up plaque outside proclaims Nasik/Dhule depending on the broadcast. This creates the vibes necessary for the differentiation,' he concludes with a smile.

We part with the understanding that the nimbleness and cost-consciousness of the private radio stations is something AIR would take a long time to match.

The interview does, however, also ignite hope.

The demographic clearly shows that the eighteen- to thirty-five-year-old segment, however influential it may be in consumption patterns, is still 24 per cent of the population, with 35 per cent being above thirty-five years of age and even those in the sixty-plus segment beginning to seek fresh experiences. They display consumption patterns similar to those many years younger; hence, the market no longer peaks at the thirty-five-year age bracket. This age group does not connect with the perennially high-energy style of private FM channels and considers the 'contemporary hits' to be cacophony. Therefore, it constitutes a niche and viable listener segment for AIR.

Also, within the eighteen to thirty-five age bracket, many take a keen interest in poetry, Indian classical music, ghazals, etc. Check out the crowd at any major Indian music concert, mushaira, kavi sammelan or dance concert and you will find a large percentage of the audience consists of young people. A significant part of this age group either stays away from today's contemporary music or finds a space in its mindset for both. Either way, there is a space for private radio stations and AIR.

If there is space for AIR, how does it propose adapting to the changing scenario to claim that space? What is the way forward? These are the questions to which we now seek answers.

'The way forward lies in taking the digital route,' Javadekar tells us as we sit across him again in his tastefully done up bungalow in Tughlaq Lane, in the Lutyens' zone in New Delhi. 'Digitization of the archives has been going on as a process for almost fourteen to fifteen years,' he says, 'but it is only in the last three or four years that it has gathered speed. Digitization has two aspects: preserving what we have and transmitting this content via digital media to increase its reach. Of course, currently created content must be broadcast digitally while simultaneously storing it for posterity. I am happy that AIR is doing both and many innovative schemes are being implemented to make sure this is done effectively.'

He cites the example of uploading digitalized content on YouTube and the launch of the Free Dish and the NewsOnAir app for mobile devices as the way forward.

'The views of the old programmes of AIR are so high that YouTube pays us ₹3 crore because of them,' he says.

We meet the deputy director-general of the central archives, Anshuman Rai, to explore the archives. A tall, bearded, soft-spoken engineer in his early fifties, he has held his current position with AIR for two of his thirty years in AIR.

We ask him what content the archives have and his answer fascinates us.

AIR possesses a national treasure—a complete map of the nation's cultural, social and political life from the '20s onwards. He takes us to the library, which has miles and miles of tapes systematically stored in a temperature and humidity-controlled environment. We are overwhelmed as he reels off what the tapes contain.

'No one has ever counted the length of the programming available within the archives,' says Rai. The Prasar Bharati website puts the figure at about 17,000 hours of programming, although many sources estimate it is almost one lakh hours.

'More significant than the quantitative aspect is the nature of the content,' Rai tells us as we sit in his aesthetically set up office in Akashvani Bhavan.

He tells us it is the single largest repository of Indian music, with the rarest of rare recordings in north and south Indian music genres preserved for posterity.

So whether it is Ustad Bade Ghulam Ali Khan singing '*Hari Om Tatsat*', Pandit D.V. Paluskar singing '*Thumak Chalat Ramchandra*', M.S. Subbulakshmi enchanting listeners with her '*Aliveni Endu Cheyvu*' or Siddheshwari Devi mesmerizing listeners with a tappa of the Benaras gharana—the archives have them all. The list of recordings available reads like a showcase of the who's who of Indian music. Rare recordings of Pandit Ravi Shankar, Ustad Ali Akbar Khan, Ustad Abdul Halim Jaffer Khan, Ustad Vilayat Khan, Ustad Alla Rakha Khan, Pandit Ram Narayan, Pandit Shivkumar Sharma, Pandit Bhajan Sopori, Ustad Amjad Ali Khan and Lalgudi Jayaraman are amongst those available in the archives. Besides this, Pandit Jasraj, Pandit Bhimsen Joshi, and younger vocalists like Ulhas Kashalkar, Kaushiki Chakraborty, and Jayateerth Mevundi all have recorded for AIR and have their performances stored here. He says that Jagjit Singh's ghazals, Aziz Ahmed Warsi's qawwalis and numerous folk forms nestle together in the archives.

He adds, 'These archives are in addition to the Vividh Bharati archives in Mumbai, which has film and light music dating from the pre-Independence era to date.'

We realize that these archives would be ideal if anyone wanted to research the evolution of great musicians as artistes. The researcher would find recordings of almost all of them at various times.

Rai continues, 'Besides this, programmes on Indian folk culture also abound and interviews with artistes and scholars about different facets of India's vast cultural diversity find great representation here. In addition, works of eminent writers in the dramatized form are preserved here.'

'We undertook a campaign for recording folk songs sung at festivals and on occasions like births, naming ceremonies, weddings, etc., from all over India. We put them together in a programme called *Sanskar Geet*. As a result, we have a collection of over 2,000 such songs and have proactively contributed to ensuring that the legacy is not lost,' Rai proclaims proudly.

We scan the archives to find a playlist of a hundred speeches by Gandhiji, speeches of Dr B.R. Ambedkar, Dr Rajendra Prasad and Sarojini Naidu in the constituent assembly and numerous speeches of Prime Ministers and Presidents of the country.

Stalwarts from the world of business are not neglected either and numerous audio biographies and interviews with those who shaped the country's industrial landscape also find space here. For example, an hour-long interview with J.R.D. Tata is something everyone from Javadekar and Vempati to our friends in AIR had told us to seek out when in the archives.

We turn to Rai to find out what AIR is doing with this treasure.

'First and foremost, there is a need to preserve it lest this rich heritage gets lost to the ravages of time,' he explains, 'But that is not enough. It has to be presented to people to engage with and relish. There is no point in letting it lie in an air-conditioned crypt—unheard and unsung.'

He explains that with the first objective in mind, a digitization programme was started in 2004 and continued to grow under different verticals. In 2018, a separate vertical was created for this activity, and the disparate verticals were brought under a common umbrella called 'Prasar Bharati Archives', the unit he currently heads. He tells us that the drive gathered speed in 2019 and his section has digitized almost 95 per cent of all the available content. He informs us that the balance of 5 per cent was too far gone to salvage, but attempts are being made to convert it by involving specialized agencies.

We ask him how the listeners access the archives and he explains that his department uploads all the digitized content on four YouTube channels, viz., DD Cinema, DD Bharti, Prasar Bharati Archives and AIR Ragam. The last two carry content from AIR and the first two are from Doordarshan. We go to each of these and at random, search for clips of various genres. Searching for Mahatma Gandhi's speeches, for instance, displays multiple options and each clip shows at least 2,000 to 5,000 views. Similarly, searching the Ragam or classical music channel shows many uploaded clips with relatively fewer but a steady and rising listenership. This kind of listenership for unheard-of content is a big thing.

'People are beginning to notice the content.' He tells us that there are often requests from movie and documentary filmmakers or producers of content for OTT platforms for permission to use these as part of their creations. 'We charge them for it and the trend is only growing.'

His mobile phone rings and, seeing the name of the caller, he puts it on speaker mode, enabling us to listen in. It is a documentary producer from Mumbai asking for an appointment to fly to Delhi to discuss the usage of a clip in her production. He tells her to hear the clip on YouTube and come over only for a review and contract finalization.

'See, this is what I was talking about,' he smiles cheerfully as he explains what else is planned.

'Seeing the interest in the uploaded content and the regular stream of enquiries we have been getting, a new policy has been formulated. We are now listing our digital assets and offering a menu for use in content creation. We will send this to various OTT channels, content creators, etc., ask them to choose any they might require and then ask them to bid for them. So instead of passively waiting for some creators to discover some clips they may want, we will actively offer the list to them, making the likelihood of enquiries coming in much higher.'

All this is very positive, but what disturbs us is that the subscriber base of the archive channels is relatively low by today's standards. The two channels together have a subscriber base of just 2.12 lakh. We again connect with Samir Kumar, the ever-smiling, affable and exceptionally talented ex-head of PBNS and DP, the organization set early in the tenure of Vempati to work on enhancing existing digital assets and creating new ones. An IIT and IIM alumnus, he is a former investment banker with a reputation for turning around many sick companies. He quit a lucrative international career spanning almost two decades to return to India and 'try to make a difference'. Joining the RSS-backed news agency Hindusthan Samachar as CEO on a token salary of ₹1, he left to join Prasar Bharati to take up the responsibility of setting up PBNS. Unfortunately, the dream ended with the unit closing down after his mentor, Vempati, who had placed a lot of confidence in him and his young team, left after his tenure as CEO. The empire struck back and all PBNS offices were closed in rapid succession. He now runs his own media agency and such was the loyalty of the staffers of PBNS and DP to Samir that most left their government jobs to join him. We ask him about the closure and his resignation. Though disappointed, he is glad he got the opportunity because his work exposed him to a new field and governmental operations and enabled him to effect many changes that set the bar for future administrators.

'The pace may slow down,' he says, 'but the changes we made will continue to dictate the agenda.'

We ask him about the work done on the social media handles of Prasar Bharati and he introduces us to Manish Verma. Manish is a tall young man with many private sector assignments under his belt. He was the digital assets manager in PBNS and DP and now works with Samir in his media house, Cliq India.

'It was all a work in progress when we left,' he states. 'Before we came in, all the stations were uploading content on to their YouTube channels and though they were sincere about what they were doing, they did not have the necessary skill set to do it to engage people in the virtual world.'

He explains that they conducted training sessions for staff at various stations, teaching them how to assign the correct keywords to the titles, create the right thumbnails, etc., to make listeners notice the uploaded pieces. Tulika Bishnoi, also an ex-PBNS staffer who has since joined Samir, gives the example of the DD National channel of Doordarshan on which they worked directly.

'We cleaned up the channel using all the techniques to increase engagement in the digital world and promoted the channel on our social media handles. As a result, the channel, which had a subscriber base of 0.9 million subscribers, built up since inception, grew to …' she stops mid-sentence and asks us to guess what it is now. She waits for our guesstimate and seeing the blank smiles on our faces, opens the site on her mobile and thrusts it towards us. We are stunned that the base is now 5.66 million—a more than five-fold increase in two years. Her enthusiasm is infectious and so when she tells us that they were also working with AIR channels, we feel reassured that with time, if the good work continues, their listenership will see a similar rise.

'The subscriber base does not fully reveal the listenership,' Manish explains. 'Quite a few listeners listen from the NewsOnAir mobile application and they do not subscribe to the channels since that option is unavailable unless you log in to YouTube.'

Hearing of the NewsOnAir app sets us off on the path of looking at how this was set to revive the radio listening habit.

We recollect Vempati telling us that radio would not only survive but would thrive, just that the mode of delivery would change. It would become linear, with platforms like YouTube, mobile apps and websites delivering a seamless experience and making content accessible across devices.

'This is the single biggest game-changer in the race to restore AIR to its pre-eminent position,' Vempati had told us. 'You know why the telegram and the telex have gone out and not returned, but radio has? In a small way it is because of the car radio, and very largely, with unlimited potential, because of the smartphone.'

When radio listenership started falling in the 1990s, the car radio undoubtedly gave the first fillip to its revival. By the 2000s, it was an essential accessory and car companies often mentioned the quality of their radio set with other features like engine capacity, safety, etc. People listen to the radio while driving to work or when stuck in traffic jams, and with roads getting better and the number of cars multiplying, listenership via car radios increased. With car owners constituting only a tiny percentage of the population, this effect remained small though significant.

A much more enormous contribution over the last few years, Vempati had told us, has been that of the mobile phone and its suitability to deliver radio transmissions. This breakthrough technology reduced the radio from being a bulky, stand-alone device to a handy application—the radio suddenly became cool again. The radio has the unique advantage of seamlessly integrating into the phone and online spaces that its predecessors didn't. The radio receivers can be embedded into mobile phones and vehicles and don't add to the cost while adding to the entertainment. This makes the phone a stand-alone, on-the-go entertainment accessory everybody needs.

With some estimates suggesting over seventy-four crore smartphones in the hands of a 140 crore population, the number of listeners that AIR can reach through the mobile app far exceeds what stand-alone radio sets or even car radio sets can ever think of reaching. However, the projections are still more interesting. It is estimated that the population of India will peak at 150 crores by 2040 and the number of smartphones will equal it. With that many potential radio sets, this medium is now the prime focus of all broadcasters.

AIR stepped into this space in 2016 by designing in-house an app called NewsOnAir. It offered news, features and music on a single platform. It was, however, not pushed aggressively and saw only nominal downloads for the first three years. It was only when Prasar Bharati launched the PBNS and DP in 2019 that the cause of the app was taken up in earnest.

'We recognized the app's potential in offering articles and op-eds, radio content and television in one place on the mobile and decided to promote it as part of the digital push. So when Manish joined us, this was one of the first tasks we allotted to him,' says Samir Kumar.

At the end of 2021, the app, at the click of a button, gave listeners access to 259 radio stations (as of January 2022) besides showing news articles and television programmes. It also grants access to archival content to those interested. In addition, a NewsOnAir website was also launched to ensure that the news was available on desktops and laptops to enable greater reach. However, there is some confusion since there is a newsonair.gov.in site from the News Services Division of AIR and another one called Newsonair.com from PBNS, which has the AIR news plus news uploaded by PBNS and Doordarshan. We mark it as a point to investigate later.

The results of this are for all to see. Listeners downloaded the app more than two million times till January 2022 and had a listenership of twenty million in that month. Furthermore, November and

December 2021, and January 2022 consistently added two million listeners to its base.

'This was the fastest-growing listener base for any platform ever and we expected it to reach five million downloads by December 2023. As we tweaked it further, added features, rebranded it and promoted it across media, we were targeting ten million downloads by 2024,' says Samir Kumar. 'Since the content is accessible from almost everywhere globally and as the downloads go up, the reach will be many times that of stand-alone radio sets. As a result, the monetization opportunities will also exponentially increase, helping the cause of financial self-sufficiency.'

We turn our attention to the app we had downloaded on our mobile phones when Vempati had first talked to us about it. It is virtually like being let into a wonderland.

The screen opens up to news headlines taken from AIR news from just an hour ago to two days back. There are a variety of languages to read these and when we check out the major Indian languages, we find that instant translations are available. All headlines bear the prominent tag of AIR news. In addition, we see live radio, radio magazines and news podcasts.

When we click on Live Radio, it blows our minds. State-wise, the 259 radio stations we had only heard of are listed below. Depending on your language preference, you can scroll down state-wise and choose the radio station you want to listen to.

'Belong to Markapur in Andhra Pradesh? Or Pasighat in Arunachal or Diphu in Assam? Did you grow up hearing radio stations from Ahwa in Gujarat, Chaibasa in Jharkhand, Devikulam in Kerala or Kavaratti in Lakshadweep? Wherever you are now, if you want to connect to your roots, listen to the news from your hometown or connect with its festivals and music—all you have to do is download this app and tap on the screen to get these in digital quality,' says Manish proudly.

We recollect Yunus Khan's comment when he spoke about the app.

'Imagine a soldier sitting on the Tibet border and tapping a screen on the app to listen to songs from his hometown. Would it ever have been possible before? Please think of the tremendous boost it will be to his morale because of the connection he will feel with his hometown.'

We sure can, but we wonder if the 'anywhere' means 'anywhere in India' or if that general statement means most of India. So we ask Samir Kumar and he laughs aloud and says neither answer is correct. 'Anywhere means anywhere in the whole world.'

'Do people tune in to the app from around the world?' we ask Samir, trying to judge its popularity. He quotes from a document that shows the app's reach.

We realize that the app reaches the Indian diaspora worldwide in eighty-five countries, with Fiji topping the number of users, followed by Australia, the United States, Canada, New Zealand, Ireland, United Kingdom, Japan, Spain and UAE. Spain comes as a surprise. We later discover that many Punjabis work in the vineyards in Spain and can imagine the smiles that would light up their faces on hearing Vividh Bharati belt out their favourite songs as they toil under the Spanish sun. Surprisingly, Gujarati also figures among the top languages Indians hear on the radio in Spain. We aren't sure why, but let it be: we are glad that someone, somewhere, is smiling because of the app.

We also discovered that the FM channels of Delhi are heard, amongst others, in the Cook Islands and Tonga, and Punjabi channels are listened to in Finland!

The listener's demographic comes as a surprise—37 per cent are between eighteen and forty-four years of age and only 21 per cent are above sixty-five. Manish tells us that the young are the fastest-growing segment and will soon be the largest. So much for the theory that the young only want contemporary hit radio.

The details of India are enlightening too and we find that Pune, Bengaluru, Delhi NCR, Hyderabad and Mumbai lead the way. The top ten cities account for 53 per cent of the listeners, indicating that the listenership is evenly distributed all over the country. Another exciting fact is that channels from the eastern part of India figure among five of the top ten heard in Delhi NCR. This is because many students from the Northeast live in the city and they access their home stations like Itanagar, Gangtok, Zoavi, Shillong and Agartala from the app.

'The app helps us identify programmes that no one is listening to and they can then be discontinued or merged with other programmes,' Vempati had told us. So, his logic behind the rationalizing of programmes begins to make sense.

We wonder why NewsOnAir is not being extensively promoted.

'It is a work in progress and many changes need to be made before it is extensively promoted,' Samir clarifies.

'The interface itself is more than six years old and in the fast-paced internet world, that is practically a lifetime,' says Manish. However, many new features were planned and the app's navigation was being made more accessible and less cluttered. These changes and a freshly designed interface should have debuted in mid-2022, but the change of reins seems to have jinxed all that, as the interface on date is the same as we initially saw it to be.

NewsOnAir is a complete AIR app, yet the feel of the name is as if it is only for radio news. We ask everyone from Vempati to Samir to Manish and Tulika, but almost everyone is non-committal, only saying that a name change is being considered. Behl, our journo friend, later tells us that a turf war between the 'Air app' and the 'News app', which merged to create this one, had caused this name to emerge. We chuckle as we realize that no one wants to say that.

We have also heard much about Free Dish, possibly the world's largest DTH (direct-to-home) infotainment platform. Our search for it leads us to Doordarshan Bhavan on Copernicus Marg. We meet the affable S.K. Verma, deputy director-general, responsible for the Free Dish programme and its commercial outreach.

Free Dish is a platform through which those with the dish and set-top box get free lifelong access to television and radio programming. All they have to do is pay for the hardware as a one-time payment, for which the government has fixed a nominal price of approximately ₹2,000 with minor regional variations.

'Initially, we had those huge dishes transmitting programming for television, which were only installed at TV stations and required a huge capital outlay, space and intensive maintenance,' Verma informs us. 'Moreover, this did not cover 100 per cent of the population since there were remote areas where it was not economically feasible to have stations for small populations. In other cases, there were problems with access and terrain. Therefore, when this technology came in, whereby a small dish and a set-top box could provide crystal clear reception, we adopted and promoted it.'

The scheme, launched in 2004 with thirty-three television channels, now beams 167 television channels and forty-eight radio channels nationwide. An estimated four-and-a-half crore set-top boxes in the country give the platform a combined base of over twenty crore people. It also hosts private channels which bid for the slots available and contributed an amount of ₹760 crore in 2021–22, around 60–70 per cent of the total revenue of Prasar Bharati.

No statistics are available for what percentage of Free Dish subscribers listen to radio via it. However, it stands to reason that as most Free Dish installations are either in rural households or lower-income families in cities, they would not spend on a radio set if the reception is available on Free Dish. So even if the percentage were small, the numbers would be huge. We come away convinced that Free Dish is performing admirably as an additional outreach method.

What we have been discussing till now has been the delivery and dissemination of content. Undoubtedly, AIR sits on a goldmine of content and some incredible content is also being created at various radio stations. We seek to know how the content could change with the advent of the latest technologies.

One of the ideas being considered is that of visual radio. We wonder what that means—how can radio be visual?

Vaibhavi Jahagirdar, a young ex-staffer at PBNS and DP, explains, 'Radio features and magazines are created with a lot of effort. Extensive research is carried out and experts carefully write a script. They also add music, edit it and record the narrative in a mellifluous voice. When we disseminate it digitally via the app or the website, what is visible is just a fixed slide as the voice-over goes on. The idea behind visual radio is to add videos and other visuals to the narrative so that when it is consumed digitally, it becomes more appealing. The national data management system would also be ideal since we can go hyperlocal to collect the visuals.'

The ability to listen to the radio on the mobile app is a beautiful innovation. It will undoubtedly add to the listenership because of the sheer number of mobile phones in the hands of the citizens because, as Vempati says, 'No one wants to lug multiple devices around.' However, it is ultimately dependent on internet connectivity. Also, though access through social media platforms is a value addition, it puts AIR at the mercy of the opaque algorithms of the platforms. Hence, both reach and autonomy are limited. Another technological advancement has now come to the forefront, which will be hugely disruptive to all existing data transmission modes and from which radio, amongst others, will immensely benefit. We meet Vempati once more to decode this technology.

The rendezvous is set up in a popular five-star hotel's coffee shop and we are there well before time, not wanting to miss out. Vempati arrives just three minutes late but has kept us in the loop by sending messages saying he was delayed. He apologizes for the non-existent delay and we settle down for coffee as he sips his masala tea.

'The new technology of direct-to-mobile will change the rules of broadcasting worldwide. And for once,' he says, the excitement writ large on his face, 'we are not following anyone but coming on board as it is unrolled worldwide.'

Developed by Saankhya Labs and IIT Kanpur in association with Prasar Bharati and the department of telecommunication, it is a technology that entirely bypasses the internet and beams programmes directly to the mobile handset. With the installation of a small chip, every mobile phone becomes a radio and TV receiver set on which we can beam down audio, video and data. Ultimately, every smartphone may come with an inbuilt chip and much like a camera, each smartphone user will have a radio in their hands. Interactive and localized content and buying small amounts of data will be possible.

'You could easily buy a ticket and watch a cricket match or concert,' Vempati tells us.

He adds that a public service broadcaster could broadcast citizen-centric information using the technology. It could combat fake news, issue emergency warnings and help in disaster management. This is apart from the broadcast of live news, sports and other entertainment. When we ask him about the 'when' of it, he tells us that a MOU is about to be signed with IIT for its rollout.

That radio has a future is established in our minds now.

We talk to Shyam Parekh, who once was an editor for a prominent newspaper and is currently building an app focused mainly on local news. He says, 'While television and other screens will continue to be ubiquitous, the power of radio is not just increasing, there is an ever-increasing realization of its power.'

Adds Jumana Shah, who worked as a journalist with newspaper and television, 'Local creators have huge advantages over network talent. Even local news is becoming more and more popular,' she adds. 'They breathe a material consequence for the stories they speak and principally, they are considered dependable. During the pandemic, local broadcasters have only become more important. People trust radio, especially AIR, and therefore it will always win,' she concludes.

We try to understand why news is still not allowed to be broadcast by private radio stations in India. As the matter is pending in the Supreme Court, most people don't want to discuss it. The private channels claim that allowing them to broadcast news will completely change the dynamic and landscape of radio journalism. It will happen sooner than later, is what most tell us. However, the primary issue of reliability will remain. Suppose private radio stations were permitted to broadcast the news. Would the 'revenue only' model take a hit on revenue for cross-checking a fact, or will they become like the TRP-driven television stations where all forms of noise pass as news? We are inclined to think that it is with the AIR that the news is really 'safe'.

On whether newer apps will take over the space belonging to radio, Sunil Gupta clarifies that radio continues to be the most accessed form of audio entertainment despite technology. He tells us a survey revealed that 70 per cent of consumers of audio infotainment listened to the radio, while the share of Spotify, to our surprise, was less than 50 per cent.

The rise in listening to the radio and other audio services on connected devices also creates new commercial opportunities in digital audio advertising placed into streamed or downloaded audio content, including radio, on-demand music services and podcasts.

In the immediate future, audio is predicted to remain a vibrant and exciting sector with interesting new developments in the pipeline, such as voice control, seamlessly changing locations and direct-to-mobile broadcasting. Many other things, like streaming the most pertinent version of an advertisement to each listener and increasing use of 3D binaural sound to deliver a more immersive audio advertising experience, were relevant.

The thought that digital disruption has eroded 'traditional' media's reach and relevance is one of the biggest misconceptions about technology. Mobile apps, Alexa skills and social media have expanded the space and opportunity for engagement, even with traditional media.

'It's all about APPortunities,' a radio veteran and a technology buff said succinctly.

How AIR handles this opportunity will be crucial to its future role in the broadcast pantheon.

A vital concern that continues to gnaw at our optimism is the concern about the low generation of new content. With the number of programming staff going down, new programmes have drastically decreased. As a result, replays of old programmes now take up a fairly large chunk of broadcasting time and if the trend continues, it could be the Achilles heel of AIR. How AIR tackles the creativity roadblock will largely determine its future.

To survive and thrive, AIR will not only have to become nimbler, continue to increase its interface with technology, significantly improve its marketing and address its staff-related issues but it will have to do all this while not losing sight of creativity in programming. A tall order indeed and yet at the end of our journey of this book, all this seems doable and possible.

'AIR is like an aircraft carrier,' Vempati says. 'It carries enormous firepower and can strike far and wide, but it is a lumbering giant and changing its direction requires tremendous energy and takes time.'

This aircraft carrier has started turning around and we cross our fingers and pray that it will emerge to be in complete command of the ocean waves in the years to come.

Author's Musings:
Vikrant Pande

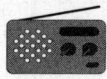

AIR HAD BEEN AN INTEGRAL PART OF MY GROWING-UP YEARS and the default channel I heard whenever I wanted to listen to the radio. Some programmes on Vividh Bharati were my favourites, as they are for millions. My brother was in the army and I have a special attachment to *Jaimala*, which is meant for our soldiers. I often hear the afternoon programme *Sakhi Saheli*, which gives a great glimpse into Indian women's thoughts. Some of the hosts' household tips are worth implementing at home and I listen to the programme whenever possible. Though I don't play any instruments, I like music and regularly listen to *Sangeet Sarita*.

Childhood memories of lying in the open air in the courtyard of our house in a public sector township in Bihar, and watching my parents tune into AIR Bombay to listen to their favourite plays, remain with me. So does the voice of Datta Kulkarni, Neelesh's father, reading the Marathi news. It was the only lesson in Marathi pronunciation and diction as we didn't have many Marathi-speaking households where we stayed in Bihar and hence there was no one to whom we could benchmark our articulation.

My friends laughed at me when I carried a transistor on the train for the long journey during summer semester breaks, travelling from Baroda, where I went to college, to Kolkata, where my father was then posted, at Haldia. The transistor was a constant companion that entertained not just me but all those co-passengers who crowded the second-class compartments. Competition of who would guess the song within ten seconds of its start was a terrific 'timepass' and we played that game for hours. On AIR, we got introduced to the lyricists, music directors and not just the singer. Thanks to AIR, I am familiar with old 'bhule bisre' songs like Pankaj Mullick's *Duniya Rang Rangeeli Baba*' to name just one. Sadly, even the singer's name is not mentioned by most private radio channels today. Later, when travelling for work in rural Bengal, with most areas having no power at night, I would have the transistor and its national programme of music as my lullaby to lull me into sleep in the sweaty, humid atmosphere.

Many of us who have memories of the '71 war with Pakistan would remember how we would eagerly await and listen to the news for updates. Of course, many people would tune in to the BBC, but it was always AIR for me.

It has always been fascinating to hear the AIR songs while buying vegetables in the mandi, visiting a local tailor or sitting in a haircutting salon. The radio softly playing in the background while the tailors work with their sewing machines is, to date, a common sight.

The fascinating aspect of our journey in researching this book on AIR was meeting with and talking to over a hundred amazing people from 2022 to 2024. It was touching to see senior newscasters, commentators, actors and musicians admitting they owe their fame to the opportunity they got on AIR and hearing them speak of it with pride, gratitude, humility and reverence.

It is encouraging to see AIR emerging from merely a public broadcaster to a genuinely independent and profitable entity that is making waves worldwide.

Author's Musings:
Neelesh Kulkarni

FOR ME, THE BOOK'S JOURNEY WAS ABOUT OPENING A BOX FULL of pleasant memories.

Memories of hours glued to the transistor set listening to the commentary of the cricket test matches. Memories of the radiogram displayed prominently in the drawing room and the seniors in the family tuning into the commentary of the Republic Day parade. Memories of an uncle who had once studied in London, sitting back in his armchair, as soft strains of Beethoven or Bach drifted across from the Telefunken radio set.

Memories of accompanying my father to AIR's studios to participate in the children's programme. Memories of mothers and aunts animatedly discussing whether the song that had climbed up to the first paaydaan or step in the *Binaca Geetmala* on Radio Ceylon deserved to be there. Memories of a cynical neighbourhood aunt haughtily proclaiming that the whole setup was fixed and that she had heard it from a friend in Bombay.

Memories of sitting in darkened homes during war times, listening to the news to find out the latest position on the border and breaking out in applause on hearing that our brave soldiers had captured one more enemy post. Memories of breaking into peals of laughter when the news from Radio Jhutistan (a parody of Radio Pakistan) came on during war times.

Memories of dedicating songs on Yuvavani to that 'girl in the yellow skirt' on the university special, not having the courage to put one's name to it and signing it off with 'an unknown admirer'. Memories of the heart beating rapidly in the university special the next day as she got in, wondering if she had heard it and if she had guessed who had requested it. Memories of going in to record an episode of *In the Groove* for Yuvavani and coming back totally smitten with the youthful producer, who incidentally went on to be the director general of AIR.

Multiple memories like these had crowded my mind when I embarked on this journey of writing the story of AIR with Vikrant. The memories drove my desire to chronicle them for posterity so that future generations would know what a phenomenon AIR was.

The journey was as fascinating as the memories of the good, languid times were fragrant, and the feelings it brought forth were mind-blowing.

There is an incredible feeling of entering the studios of AIR for the first time after a gap of over forty or fifty years. The fantastic feeling of waiting for one's car, standing under the same canopy of Broadcasting House where Pandit Ravi Shankar once stood waiting for his own. The proud feeling when telling the receptionist issuing entry passes for Broadcasting House, '*Arre tumhare paida hone se pehle se hum yahan aate hain* (I have been coming here since before you were even born)', in answer to his question of whether we knew our way around inside. All these feelings contributed to making the journey of writing this book more emotional than cerebral. However, the numerous dedicated individuals we met during the journey added immeasurable value to it and hence, to the book.

Fan moments abounded. Calling up Sushil Doshi to talk about commentary, sitting across from Sunit Tandon talking of his English news reading days and listening to Chhaya Ganguli hum her award-winning song '*Aapki Yaad Aati Rahi Raat Bhar*' on request—each was a moment to be treasured.

The real stars of the saga, though, were the ones who were not the stars in the public eye and yet, within their circles, were stars in their own right—multiple images of dedication and love for the medium crowd the mind.

The image of a Manoj Atri, during the lockdown, enacting slithering dance moves to make his daughter chuckle so that she could record the title song of a children's storytelling series in the right mood. The image of Novy Kapadia, the noted sportscaster, ailing and wheelchair-bound, having his attendant hold the telephone to his ears so that he could answer our questions without tiring. The image of Pandit Naresh Malhotra proudly explaining how the AIR selection process is impartial. The image of Basudha Banerji rushing around to get payments to Ruskin Bond cleared in time; him remembering her after many years and agreeing to record stories in his voice during the lockdown.

What came across was their tremendous dedication to the craft, immense love for the medium and pride in working for AIR.

There was also a sinking feeling as fault lines emerged somewhere along the way. AIR's slow working pace, the attractions of the catchier FM channels, the heartbreaking stories of no-promotion careers, staff crunches, programmes being axed, mounting losses, cadre imbalances and an apparent loss of listenership all contributed to it.

However, when we probed into the reasons behind these, the silver lining to the clouds started emerging. Expenses were being controlled and no jobs were being axed. Promotion-less careers were a tragic reality, but the concern was being addressed.

Technology was being harnessed and the footprint of AIR was not shrinking but was growing nationally and internationally.

Many challenges remain and the factors dragging AIR from achieving its fullest potential continue to cling to it and could still capsize it, but there is hope.

Hope that a leaner, nimbler organization will emerge over time. Hope that creativity will continue to remain centre stage. Hope that indigenous cultures will continue to find a saviour in AIR and that the full-throated embracing of technology will propel it forward.

By the time we came to the end of the book, nostalgia had merged with hope and created a heady cocktail.

So, download the app and tune in to your favourite stations wherever you are. Happy listening!

About the Authors

Vikrant Pande has translated fifteen Marathi bestsellers into English. His translation of Girish Kuber's book *Tatayan* (*The Tatas: How a Family Built a Business and a Nation*) won the prestigious Gaja Capital Business Book Prize in 2019, and his translation of Ranjit Desai's *Shriman Yogi* (*Shivaji: The Great Maratha*) is a bestseller. Pande's book *In the Footsteps of Rama: Travels with the Ramayana*, co-authored with Neelesh Kulkarni, was translated into three languages and is now being made into an OTT travel series. His book on the history of the State Bank of India, *The SBI Story: Two Centuries of Banking*, has been well received. He has translated and written original pieces for Storytel, an audio book company. Pande is a graduate of IIM Bangalore.

Neelesh Kulkarni is a management graduate from the Faculty of Management, Delhi University, who quit the corporate world in 1985 to start his own company. He is a theatre and voice-over artiste with over fifty years of experience, an avid reader and traveller, a poet, a cricket commentator and a public-speaking coach. His previous book, *Uprising: The Liberation of Dadra and Nagar Haveli*, has received favourable reviews from critics and readers alike. He lives in Delhi with his artist wife. This is his fifth book.

ALSO BY VIKRANT PANDE AND NEELESH KULKARNI

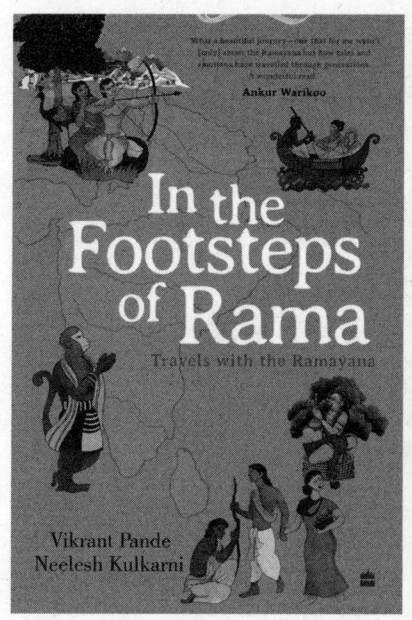

'In this book, Vikrant and Neelesh set out to cover a journey that many Indians traverse in their imagination ... [They] find that the ancient story of love and adventure continues to inspire a civilization ...'
Sanjeev Sanyal, economist, urban theorist and author

Vikrant Pande and Neelesh Kulkarni's quest to retrace the route of Rama's fabled travels during his years in exile began with their trying to locate Chitrakoot on the map and realizing that they had little idea where it was. Curious about the places mentioned in the Ramayana, they set off on a voyage of their own, following in Rama's footsteps, from Ayodhya to the Dandakaranya forest and Panchvati (near Nashik), and on to Kishkindha (close to Hampi), Rameshwaram and Sri Lanka. Along the way they would discover how closely the narrative of the Ramayana is linked to local folklore, and how the stories of the epic and the moral framework that binds them together still speak to the people who live on the land across which Rama, Sita and Lakshman made their journey. For the armchair traveller as well as those interested in India's cultural history, this is a wonderful book with which to revisit the world of the Ramayana.

Non-Fiction/Travelogue   HB price: ₹599
                              PB price: ₹399

HarperCollins *Publishers* India

At HarperCollins India, we believe in telling the best stories and finding the widest readership for our books in every format possible. We started publishing in 1992; a great deal has changed since then, but what has remained constant is the passion with which our authors write their books, the love with which readers receive them, and the sheer joy and excitement that we as publishers feel in being a part of the publishing process.

Over the years, we've had the pleasure of publishing some of the finest writing from the subcontinent and around the world, including several award-winning titles and some of the biggest bestsellers in India's publishing history. But nothing has meant more to us than the fact that millions of people have read the books we published, and that somewhere, a book of ours might have made a difference.

As we look to the future, we go back to that one word— a word which has been a driving force for us all these years.

Read.